Procurement for Projects

A Comprehensive Guide to Excellence in Project Sourcing and Contracting

Table of Contents

Section 1: Fundamentals of Project Procurement

1. Introduction to Procurement in Projects	5
2. The Procurement Lifecycle	10
3. Understanding Project Procurement Requirements	15
4. Procurement Strategies for Projects	21
5. Procurement Policies and Compliance	28

Section 2: Procurement Planning and Vendor Management

6. Procurement Planning	36
7. Market Analysis and Supplier Research	42
8. Supplier Prequalification and Evaluation	48
9. Request for Proposals (RFP) and Tendering Processes	55
10. Vendor Relationships and Collaboration	63

Section 3: Contracting and Negotiations

11. Contract Types and Selection	72
12. Contract Drafting and Review	80
13. Negotiation Skills for Project Procurement	87
14. Managing Contract Risks	93
15. Closing Contracts and Final Deliverables	99

Section 4: Execution and Control

16. Procurement Execution and Order Management	107
17. Monitoring and Controlling Procurement Activities	114
18. Procurement Cost Management	121
19. Change Management in Procurement	128

Section 5: Advanced Topics in Project Procurement

20. Risk Management in Procurement	136
21. Sustainable Procurement Practices	144
22. Technology in Project Procurement	152
23. Global Procurement in Projects	160
24. Procurement Lessons from Real-World Projects	167
Section 6: Conclusion and Future Trends	174
25. The Future of Procurement in Project Management	175

Section 1: Fundamentals of Project Procurement

1. Introduction to Procurement in Projects

Definition and Scope of Project Procurement
Procurement in the context of projects refers to the process of acquiring goods, services, or works from external sources necessary for completing a project. Unlike routine procurement, which supports ongoing operations, project procurement is goal-specific, aligning with the unique objectives, constraints, and timelines of a particular project. It encompasses activities such as identifying needs, selecting vendors, negotiating contracts, managing supplier relationships, and ensuring timely delivery of quality products or services.

The scope of project procurement varies based on the complexity and scale of the project. For instance, in construction, procurement may involve sourcing raw materials, hiring subcontractors, and securing heavy machinery. In IT projects, it might focus on acquiring software, licensing, or consulting services. Regardless of the industry, effective procurement ensures that resources align with project requirements, cost considerations, and timelines.

A critical aspect of project procurement is its strategic alignment with the project goals. It goes beyond transactional purchasing to involve planning, collaboration, and risk management. This strategic approach ensures the seamless integration of procurement activities into the overall project plan, enabling teams to deliver outcomes efficiently and effectively.

How Procurement Drives Project Success
Procurement plays a pivotal role in project success, acting as a bridge between project needs and external resources. It ensures that the right resources are acquired at the right time and cost, directly influencing the quality, budget, and timeline of a project. When executed effectively, procurement becomes a value-adding process, optimizing resource allocation and enabling project teams to focus on core activities.

One of the ways procurement drives success is by minimizing risks associated with supply chain disruptions. By carefully selecting reliable suppliers and drafting robust contracts, procurement professionals mitigate uncertainties that could derail a project. For example, in large-scale infrastructure projects, securing long-term agreements with key suppliers reduces the risk of cost escalation or delays due to material shortages.

Procurement also contributes to cost efficiency. Through competitive bidding, negotiation, and market analysis, procurement teams can identify opportunities for cost savings without compromising quality. Additionally, the integration of procurement planning with the overall project strategy helps avoid redundant expenditures and ensures that all acquisitions align with project objectives.

Collaboration is another critical factor. Procurement fosters partnerships with suppliers, promoting mutual understanding and long-term value creation. Strategic relationships often lead to innovations or process improvements that benefit both parties. For instance, a vendor may suggest a cost-effective alternative material that meets the project's specifications while reducing expenses.

Moreover, procurement ensures compliance with legal, ethical, and regulatory standards. This safeguards the project from potential legal disputes and reputational damage. Adherence to corporate procurement policies and international trade regulations is particularly vital in cross-border projects, where non-compliance could lead to costly delays or penalties.

Differences Between Routine and Project-Based Procurement
While both routine and project-based procurement involve acquiring goods and services, their objectives, processes, and challenges differ significantly. Understanding these distinctions is crucial for adapting procurement practices to the unique demands of project environments.

Routine procurement supports day-to-day operations of an organization, focusing on recurring needs such as office supplies, maintenance services, or raw materials for production. These purchases are often standardized and predictable, allowing organizations to establish long-term contracts with suppliers or leverage economies of scale. Routine procurement emphasizes efficiency, consistency, and cost control, with well-defined procedures and minimal variability.

In contrast, project-based procurement is characterized by its dynamic and goal-specific nature. Projects are temporary endeavors with distinct objectives, such as launching a new product, constructing a facility, or implementing a technological upgrade. Consequently, procurement activities must be tailored to the unique requirements of each project. This often involves extensive market research, customized contract terms, and flexible procurement strategies to accommodate evolving project needs.

One key difference lies in the level of complexity. Project-based procurement often involves high-value, non-standard items or services that require detailed specifications and close coordination with suppliers. For example, procuring a custom-designed component for a manufacturing project demands a deeper understanding of technical requirements and collaboration between engineers, procurement specialists, and suppliers.

Timelines also differ significantly. Routine procurement operates on ongoing cycles, with predictable lead times and delivery schedules. In contrast, project procurement is driven by the project schedule, requiring precise synchronization of procurement activities with project milestones. Delays in procurement can have cascading effects on the project timeline, underscoring the need for proactive planning and execution.

Additionally, the risk profile varies. Routine procurement deals with relatively stable supply chains, while project procurement often faces greater uncertainties. These may include fluctuating market prices, geopolitical risks, or vendor performance issues. Effective risk management is therefore a cornerstone of project procurement, involving strategies such as diversifying suppliers, including contingency clauses in contracts, and maintaining buffer stocks.

Financial considerations also differ. Routine procurement benefits from established budgets and economies of scale, while project procurement must balance cost-efficiency with the unique financial constraints of the project. This requires meticulous budgeting and cost-tracking throughout the procurement lifecycle to avoid budget overruns.

Despite these differences, the two types of procurement share common principles, such as the need for transparency, ethical conduct, and supplier relationship management. Organizations that excel in both routine and project procurement typically have robust processes, skilled personnel, and advanced tools to adapt to diverse procurement scenarios.

In conclusion, project procurement is a complex, dynamic process that drives project success through strategic planning, collaboration, and risk management. By understanding its scope and distinct characteristics, organizations can tailor their procurement practices to meet the unique challenges of project environments, ensuring the timely delivery of high-quality outcomes.

2. The Procurement Lifecycle

Overview of Procurement Phases: Planning, Execution, Control, and Closure

Procurement in projects is not merely about purchasing; it is a structured process that follows a lifecycle encompassing four key phases: planning, execution, control, and closure. Each phase is integral to ensuring that the procurement activities align with the project's goals, timelines, and budgets. Understanding and effectively managing this lifecycle is crucial for successful project outcomes.

Planning

Planning is the foundation of the procurement lifecycle. It involves identifying the project's procurement needs, defining requirements, and setting the framework for sourcing and vendor management. This phase begins with a thorough assessment of the project objectives and a breakdown of deliverables into manageable components, often guided by the Work Breakdown Structure (WBS).

During planning, procurement professionals develop the procurement management plan, a comprehensive document outlining the strategies, timelines, budgets, and evaluation criteria for vendor selection. This plan also defines the roles and responsibilities of the procurement team, the types of contracts to be used, and risk management strategies.

A critical part of planning is market research. Understanding supplier capabilities, pricing trends, and industry standards helps in formulating realistic expectations and identifying potential challenges. This phase also involves determining the procurement method, whether through competitive bidding, direct negotiations, or framework agreements.

Execution

The execution phase is where the plans are put into action. It starts with the solicitation process, which involves preparing and issuing Request for Proposals (RFPs), Invitations to Bid (ITBs), or Requests for Quotations (RFQs). These documents must clearly communicate the project requirements, evaluation criteria, and submission timelines to potential vendors.

Once responses are received, the procurement team evaluates bids or proposals based on predefined criteria such as cost, quality, delivery timelines, and vendor experience. This evaluation process ensures transparency and fairness, minimizing the risk of disputes.

After selecting the vendor, the next step is contract negotiation and finalization. Negotiations focus on securing favorable terms while ensuring mutual benefits for both parties. Once the contract is signed, purchase orders are issued, and the vendor begins delivering goods or services. During this phase, maintaining clear communication with vendors is vital to prevent misunderstandings and ensure alignment with project goals.

Control

The control phase ensures that procurement activities remain on track and align with the project objectives. It involves monitoring vendor performance, managing changes, and addressing any deviations or risks that may arise.

Key performance indicators (KPIs) such as delivery schedules, cost variances, and quality standards are used to measure performance. Tools like procurement dashboards and reporting systems provide real-time insights, enabling project managers to make informed decisions.

Change management is a critical component of this phase. Unexpected changes in project scope, timelines, or budgets can impact procurement activities. Effective communication between project teams and vendors is essential to manage these changes without causing significant disruptions.

Risk management also plays a significant role. Potential risks, such as supply chain disruptions or non-compliance with contractual terms, are identified and mitigated through proactive strategies. These may include diversifying suppliers, renegotiating contracts, or implementing contingency plans.

Closure
The closure phase marks the completion of procurement activities. It involves ensuring that all contractual obligations are fulfilled, payments are settled, and deliverables are accepted. This phase also includes conducting a final performance review of the vendor, documenting lessons learned, and archiving procurement records for future reference.

A formal contract closeout process is crucial to verify that all terms and conditions have been met. This includes resolving any outstanding issues, such as warranty claims or final inspections. Once all obligations are satisfied, a formal sign-off is obtained, and the contract is officially closed.

The closure phase is also an opportunity for reflection and improvement. By analyzing the successes and challenges of the procurement process, organizations can identify areas for improvement and apply these insights to future projects.

Integration of Procurement in the Project Management Process

Procurement is not an isolated function; it is deeply intertwined with the project management process. The integration of procurement into project management ensures that all sourcing activities align seamlessly with the project's objectives, timelines, and deliverables.

Procurement planning begins during the project initiation and planning phases. As project managers define objectives and scope, procurement professionals contribute by identifying the resources and suppliers needed to achieve these goals. This collaborative approach ensures that procurement considerations are factored into the project baseline.

During project execution, procurement supports key activities such as resource allocation, risk management, and stakeholder communication.

For example, delays in procurement can impact the critical path of the project schedule, necessitating close coordination between project managers and procurement teams to mitigate risks.

Integration also involves aligning procurement milestones with project phases. For instance, long-lead items that require extensive manufacturing or shipping timelines must be ordered well in advance to avoid delays. Similarly, contracts for critical services, such as engineering or installation, must be aligned with the project's execution schedule.

Communication is a cornerstone of integration. Regular updates between procurement and project teams ensure that both parties are aware of progress, challenges, and changes. This fosters a proactive approach to problem-solving and minimizes the risk of misalignment.

Moreover, the use of project management tools and techniques enhances integration. Tools like Gantt charts, critical path analysis, and project dashboards help synchronize procurement activities with the overall project plan. These tools also provide visibility into the interdependencies between procurement and other project functions, such as design, engineering, or construction.

The integration of procurement into project management also extends to stakeholder engagement. Procurement teams often interact with a wide range of stakeholders, including project sponsors, contractors, and regulatory bodies. Ensuring alignment between these stakeholders is essential for smooth project execution.

In conclusion, the procurement lifecycle is a systematic process encompassing planning, execution, control, and closure, each playing a vital role in achieving project objectives. Integrating procurement into the project management process ensures that sourcing activities align with the project's goals, timelines, and budgets, contributing to successful outcomes. Through strategic planning, effective execution, rigorous control, and reflective closure, procurement becomes a cornerstone of project success.

3. Understanding Project Procurement Requirements

Effective procurement begins with a comprehensive understanding of the project's requirements. This chapter delves into the critical aspects of identifying procurement needs, preparing detailed specifications, utilizing the Work Breakdown Structure (WBS) for procurement, and balancing the often-conflicting priorities of cost, quality, and timelines.

Identifying Needs and Preparing Detailed Specifications

Procurement needs are identified by assessing the project's scope, objectives, and deliverables. This requires close collaboration between project teams, stakeholders, and end-users to ensure that the procurement activities align with the project's overarching goals. The identification of needs is not merely about listing materials, services, or equipment but understanding their purpose, functionality, and contribution to the project.

The first step is conducting a gap analysis to determine what resources are required and what is already available. This analysis helps avoid unnecessary purchases and ensures efficient allocation of project resources. For example, a construction project might identify the need for specialized equipment, skilled labor, and raw materials after evaluating its existing inventory and workforce capabilities.

Once needs are identified, the next step is to prepare detailed specifications. Specifications are the foundation of procurement and serve as a communication tool between the buyer and suppliers. Well-defined specifications provide clarity about what is required, minimizing the risk of misinterpretation or errors during procurement.

Specifications can be categorized into two main types:

> **Functional Specifications**: These focus on the purpose and performance of the item or service. For example, specifying the load capacity of a crane required for a construction project.

Technical Specifications: These detail the exact parameters, dimensions, or materials required. For instance, a technical specification for steel bars may include tensile strength, grade, and length.

The preparation of detailed specifications involves gathering input from various stakeholders, including engineers, designers, and end-users. This ensures that all perspectives are considered and that the specifications address the project's technical and functional requirements.

The Role of the Work Breakdown Structure (WBS) in Procurement

The Work Breakdown Structure (WBS) is a hierarchical framework that divides the project into smaller, manageable components. Each component represents a deliverable or activity required to achieve the project's objectives. The WBS is an invaluable tool in procurement because it provides a clear picture of the project's needs and dependencies.

In procurement, the WBS helps in several ways:

Identifying Procurement Packages: By breaking the project into smaller parts, the WBS identifies specific procurement requirements, such as materials, equipment, or subcontracted services.

Prioritizing Procurement Activities: The WBS highlights critical components that directly impact project timelines, enabling procurement teams to prioritize sourcing for these elements.

Budget Allocation: Each WBS element is associated with a cost estimate, allowing procurement teams to allocate budgets effectively.

Risk Identification: The WBS helps identify potential procurement risks, such as long lead times for certain items or dependencies on specific vendors.

For example, in an infrastructure project, the WBS might include elements like site preparation, foundation work, structural components, and finishing tasks. Each element would have its corresponding procurement needs, such as excavation equipment for site preparation or concrete and steel for the foundation.

The integration of the WBS into procurement planning ensures that all requirements are captured and aligned with the project's scope. It also facilitates better communication between project and procurement teams, as the WBS provides a common reference point for discussing needs and timelines.

Balancing Cost, Quality, and Timelines

Balancing cost, quality, and timelines is one of the most challenging aspects of project procurement. These three factors, often referred to as the "triple constraint," are interdependent and require careful management to achieve project success.

Cost Management
Cost is a critical consideration in procurement, as it directly impacts the project's budget. Procurement teams must strive to obtain the best value for money without compromising quality or timelines. This involves negotiating favorable terms, leveraging economies of scale, and exploring alternative sourcing options.

However, a focus on cost alone can lead to suboptimal outcomes. For example, opting for the cheapest materials may result in poor quality, leading to higher repair or replacement costs in the long run. Therefore, cost considerations must always be balanced against quality and performance requirements.

Quality Assurance
Quality is a non-negotiable aspect of procurement, as it directly influences the project's outcomes. Poor-quality materials or services can lead to delays, safety risks, and increased costs due to rework or failures. To ensure quality, procurement teams must:

Specify quality standards in contracts.

Conduct supplier audits and inspections.

Include quality assurance clauses, such as warranties or penalties for non-compliance.

For instance, in an aerospace project, the quality of components must meet stringent safety and performance standards. Compromising on quality, even to save costs, could have catastrophic consequences.

Timelines and Delivery
Timely delivery of goods and services is crucial to keeping the project on schedule. Delays in procurement can disrupt project workflows, resulting in cost overruns and missed deadlines. To manage timelines effectively, procurement teams must:

Communicate clear delivery schedules to suppliers.

Include penalties for late delivery in contracts.

Monitor progress using procurement tracking tools.

Procurement teams must also account for external factors that may impact timelines, such as transportation delays, regulatory approvals, or supply chain disruptions. Building buffers into the procurement schedule can help mitigate these risks.

Balancing the Triple Constraint

Achieving a balance between cost, quality, and timelines requires a strategic approach. Trade-offs may be necessary, but they should be made in a way that minimizes risks and aligns with the project's objectives. For example, if quality is the top priority in a healthcare project, procurement teams might allocate a higher budget to source premium materials and ensure timely delivery, even if it involves expedited shipping.

Collaboration with stakeholders is essential in this balancing act. By engaging project managers, engineers, and end-users in procurement decisions, teams can make informed choices that consider all perspectives. Tools like value analysis and total cost of ownership (TCO) analysis can also aid in making balanced decisions.

In conclusion, understanding project procurement requirements is a multifaceted process that involves identifying needs, preparing detailed specifications, leveraging the WBS, and balancing cost, quality, and timelines. By adopting a structured and collaborative approach, procurement teams can ensure that sourcing activities contribute to the project's success while mitigating risks and optimizing resources.

4. Procurement Strategies for Projects

Effective procurement strategies are the cornerstone of successful project execution. They determine how resources are sourced, how suppliers are managed, and how the procurement process aligns with the project's objectives. This chapter explores key procurement strategies, the alignment of procurement with overall project strategy, and the customization of procurement approaches for different types of projects.

Key Procurement Strategies (Centralized, Decentralized, Hybrid)

The structure of procurement operations significantly impacts project outcomes. Organizations typically adopt one of three primary procurement strategies: centralized, decentralized, or hybrid. Each approach has its strengths and weaknesses and is suited to specific project and organizational needs.

Centralized Procurement Strategy

In a centralized strategy, procurement activities are managed and controlled by a single, central unit within the organization. This unit is responsible for purchasing decisions, supplier negotiations, and contract management.

The key advantages of centralized procurement include:

> **Economies of Scale**: Consolidating purchasing power allows organizations to negotiate better prices and terms with suppliers.

> **Standardization**: Centralized procurement ensures consistency in quality and specifications across projects.

> **Expertise**: A centralized team develops specialized expertise in procurement processes, leading to better decision-making.

However, centralized procurement can be less flexible and may lead to delays if the approval processes are overly bureaucratic. For instance, in a multinational organization, a centralized approach might struggle to address the specific needs of regional projects effectively.

Decentralized Procurement Strategy
In a decentralized strategy, procurement decisions are made at the project or departmental level. Each unit or project team has the autonomy to manage its own procurement activities.

The advantages of decentralized procurement include:

Flexibility: Project teams can respond quickly to specific needs and changes in project requirements.

Local Expertise: Decentralized procurement allows teams to leverage local market knowledge, which is particularly valuable in international projects.

Tailored Solutions: Procurement can be customized to meet the unique requirements of individual projects.

However, decentralized procurement can lead to challenges such as inconsistent quality, duplication of efforts, and higher costs due to the lack of consolidated purchasing power.

Hybrid Procurement Strategy
The hybrid strategy combines elements of centralized and decentralized procurement. Organizations adopting this approach centralize certain aspects of procurement, such as supplier selection and policy enforcement, while allowing individual projects to manage specific purchasing activities.

The hybrid approach offers the benefits of both centralized and decentralized strategies:

Efficiency and Flexibility: Organizations can standardize critical procurement functions while maintaining the flexibility to address project-specific needs.

Risk Mitigation: Central oversight reduces the risk of non-compliance or substandard quality.

Cost Savings: Consolidated contracts for common goods and services enable cost savings, while project teams retain control over specialized procurement.

For example, in a large-scale construction project, heavy machinery might be procured centrally to ensure uniformity and cost savings, while site-specific materials are sourced locally by the project team.

Aligning Procurement with Overall Project Strategy

Procurement is not a standalone function but an integral part of project strategy. The alignment of procurement with the overall project strategy ensures that sourcing activities contribute to achieving the project's goals, timelines, and budget constraints.

Defining Project Objectives
The first step in aligning procurement with project strategy is to clearly define the project's objectives. These objectives could include cost efficiency, timely delivery, innovation, or sustainability. For instance, in a renewable energy project, sustainability might be a primary objective, influencing the selection of suppliers and materials.

Stakeholder Collaboration
Collaboration between procurement teams and project stakeholders is essential to align goals and expectations. Regular communication ensures that procurement activities address the project's evolving needs and that stakeholders are informed of progress and potential risks.

Risk and Opportunity Assessment
Procurement teams must identify potential risks and opportunities

associated with the project. For example, sourcing from a single supplier might reduce costs but increase dependency risk. A balanced approach that mitigates risks while capitalizing on opportunities ensures that procurement supports the project's strategic objectives.

Key Performance Indicators (KPIs)

Defining KPIs for procurement activities ensures alignment with project goals. KPIs such as cost savings, on-time delivery, and supplier performance provide measurable benchmarks to assess the effectiveness of procurement strategies.

Customizing Procurement Approaches for Different Project Types

Different projects have unique characteristics that require tailored procurement approaches. Customization ensures that procurement activities are relevant, efficient, and aligned with the project's specific needs.

Capital-Intensive Projects

In projects with significant capital investments, such as infrastructure or manufacturing plants, procurement focuses on high-value items like machinery and equipment. Strategies for such projects include:

Bulk Purchasing: Negotiating long-term contracts to secure favorable pricing.

Vendor Partnerships: Building strong relationships with key suppliers to ensure reliability and support.

Risk Sharing: Using contracts that allocate risks appropriately between the buyer and suppliers.

Service-Oriented Projects

In service-driven projects, such as software development or consulting, procurement focuses on acquiring skilled labor or expertise. Key strategies include:

Prequalification: Evaluating vendors' capabilities and expertise before awarding contracts.

Flexible Contracts: Adopting time-and-material or milestone-based contracts to accommodate evolving project requirements.

Agile or Fast-Track Projects

For projects with tight timelines or agile methodologies, procurement must be highly responsive and adaptable. Strategies for these projects include:

Just-in-Time Procurement: Ensuring that materials or services are delivered exactly when needed to avoid delays.

Decentralized Decision-Making: Empowering project teams to make quick procurement decisions.

International Projects

Global projects involve cross-border procurement, which presents challenges like cultural differences, exchange rate fluctuations, and regulatory compliance. Strategies for such projects include:

Local Sourcing: Partnering with local suppliers to reduce logistics costs and ensure compliance with local regulations.

Global Framework Agreements: Establishing contracts with multinational suppliers to streamline procurement processes.

Procurement strategies must be dynamic and adaptable to meet the demands of diverse projects. By understanding the unique requirements of each project and tailoring procurement approaches accordingly, organizations can maximize efficiency, mitigate risks, and achieve strategic alignment.

In summary, the selection of procurement strategies—whether centralized, decentralized, or hybrid—plays a pivotal role in project success. Aligning procurement with project strategy and customizing approaches for different project types ensures that procurement activities drive value and support the achievement of project objectives.

5. Procurement Policies and Compliance

Procurement policies and compliance are vital components of successful project management. They establish the framework within which procurement activities are conducted, ensuring adherence to legal requirements, corporate standards, and ethical practices. This chapter explores the significance of understanding legal and regulatory frameworks, the role of corporate procurement policies in governance, and the importance of ethical considerations and anti-corruption measures.

Understanding Legal and Regulatory Frameworks

Procurement operates within a web of legal and regulatory frameworks that vary by industry, region, and project type. These frameworks provide the legal backbone for procurement contracts, transactions, and interactions with suppliers.

Contract Law and Procurement

Contracts form the basis of procurement transactions, specifying the rights, responsibilities, and obligations of all parties involved. Understanding contract law ensures that agreements are enforceable and mitigate risks of disputes. Essential elements of a procurement contract include:

> **Offer and Acceptance**: A clear proposal by one party and its unconditional acceptance by another.
>
> **Consideration**: Something of value exchanged between parties, such as goods, services, or payment.
>
> **Legal Purpose**: The contract must be for lawful activities and comply with regulations.

Failure to draft and manage contracts carefully can result in legal disputes, project delays, and financial losses.

Regulatory Compliance

Procurement must align with national and international regulations governing trade, labor, and environmental standards. Common regulatory considerations include:

Trade Regulations: Tariffs, import/export restrictions, and customs requirements that affect cross-border procurement.

Labor Laws: Ensuring suppliers comply with fair labor practices and avoid exploitation or discrimination.

Environmental Regulations: Compliance with laws promoting sustainable practices, such as minimizing waste or using eco-friendly materials.

For example, in industries like construction and pharmaceuticals, non-compliance with safety and quality regulations can lead to severe penalties and reputational damage.

Corporate Procurement Policies and Governance

Corporate procurement policies serve as internal guidelines to standardize procurement processes and ensure alignment with organizational goals. These policies are essential for maintaining consistency, efficiency, and accountability.

Standardizing Procurement Processes

Corporate procurement policies outline procedures for key activities such as supplier selection, bid evaluation, and contract management. Standardization ensures that all projects follow best practices, reducing the risk of errors or inconsistencies.

Budget Control and Financial Oversight

Procurement policies establish financial controls to prevent overspending and ensure value for money. For instance, organizations may set thresholds for purchase approvals, requiring higher-level authorization for large expenditures.

Risk Management in Procurement Governance
Effective governance includes identifying, assessing, and mitigating procurement risks. Policies often mandate the use of risk assessment tools and contingency planning to address potential issues such as supplier non-performance or market volatility.

Role of Technology in Governance
Many organizations leverage procurement software to enforce compliance with corporate policies. These tools provide visibility into procurement activities, automate approval workflows, and flag potential violations, enhancing governance efficiency.

Ethical Considerations and Anti-Corruption Measures

Ethical procurement practices build trust, protect organizational integrity, and contribute to sustainable project success. Ethical considerations encompass transparency, fairness, and accountability in all procurement activities.

Promoting Fair Competition
Procurement must ensure a level playing field for all suppliers. This involves creating clear and unbiased bid criteria, avoiding favoritism, and selecting suppliers based on merit. Fair competition not only drives better value but also fosters innovation and supplier engagement.

Transparency and Accountability
Transparency involves openly communicating procurement requirements, processes, and outcomes to stakeholders. Accountability ensures that procurement decisions are justified and can withstand scrutiny. Organizations often achieve these goals by:

Maintaining detailed records of procurement activities.

Conducting regular audits to ensure compliance.

Engaging independent reviewers for high-value contracts.

Addressing Conflicts of Interest
Procurement professionals must avoid conflicts of interest, where personal or financial interests could compromise decision-making. Corporate policies often include measures to prevent conflicts, such as mandatory disclosures and restrictions on accepting gifts from suppliers.

Anti-Corruption Measures
Corruption in procurement, such as bribery or kickbacks, undermines project success and exposes organizations to legal and reputational risks. Anti-corruption measures include:

> **Implementing a Code of Conduct**: Establishing clear guidelines for ethical behavior and consequences for violations.
>
> **Training and Awareness**: Educating procurement teams on identifying and addressing corruption risks.
>
> **Whistleblower Protections**: Encouraging employees to report unethical behavior without fear of retaliation.

International frameworks, such as the United Nations Convention Against Corruption (UNCAC), also provide guidance on combating corruption in procurement. Adhering to these standards demonstrates an organization's commitment to ethical practices.

Building a Culture of Ethics and Compliance

Ethical procurement and compliance require more than policies—they demand a cultural shift within organizations. Leaders must model ethical behavior, reward integrity, and create an environment where employees feel empowered to uphold ethical standards.

Procurement policies and compliance are critical to project success. By understanding and adhering to legal and regulatory frameworks, implementing robust corporate policies, and fostering ethical practices, organizations can mitigate risks, drive efficiency, and maintain stakeholder trust. In an increasingly complex global environment, prioritizing compliance and ethics ensures that procurement contributes not only to project goals but also to broader organizational and societal objectives.

Section 2: Procurement Planning and Vendor Management

6.Procurement Planning

Procurement planning is a critical phase in project management that lays the foundation for successful sourcing, acquisition, and delivery of goods and services. It involves creating a structured roadmap to identify procurement needs, allocate resources, and establish timelines and budgets. A robust procurement plan ensures alignment with project objectives and minimizes risks associated with delays, cost overruns, and miscommunication. This chapter explores the components of a procurement management plan, tools for scheduling and budgeting, and common pitfalls to avoid.

Creating a Procurement Management Plan

A procurement management plan is a document that outlines how procurement activities will be conducted throughout a project. It provides clarity on roles, responsibilities, timelines, and processes, ensuring that all stakeholders are aligned.

Defining Procurement Objectives

The first step in developing a procurement management plan is to define clear objectives. These objectives should align with the project's overall goals and may include ensuring cost efficiency, maintaining quality standards, and meeting delivery deadlines.

For instance, in a construction project, procurement objectives might prioritize sourcing sustainable materials while adhering to a strict timeline. Clearly defined objectives guide decision-making and set the tone for the entire procurement process.

Identifying Procurement Requirements

Understanding what needs to be procured is fundamental. This involves:

> **Itemizing Goods and Services**: Creating a detailed list of what is required for the project.

Determining Specifications: Outlining technical and functional requirements to ensure suppliers understand the expectations.

Establishing Quantities: Accurately estimating the amount of each item or service needed to avoid over- or under-procurement.

For complex projects, breaking down requirements using tools like the Work Breakdown Structure (WBS) can ensure nothing is overlooked.

Roles and Responsibilities

The procurement management plan should clearly define the roles and responsibilities of team members involved in procurement. Key roles include:

Procurement Managers: Oversee the procurement process and maintain accountability.

Project Managers: Ensure procurement aligns with project timelines and budgets.

Stakeholders: Provide input on requirements and approve critical decisions.

Clear role delineation reduces confusion and ensures accountability at each stage.

Contracting and Risk Management

The procurement plan must address how contracts will be managed and risks mitigated. This includes:

Identifying the types of contracts to be used (e.g., fixed-price, cost-plus).

Outlining a risk management strategy to address potential issues such as supplier delays or cost fluctuations.

Establishing performance metrics to measure supplier compliance.

Tools for Procurement Scheduling and Budgeting

Efficient scheduling and budgeting are essential components of procurement planning. They ensure that procurement activities are completed on time and within financial constraints.

Gantt Charts and Timelines
Gantt charts are a popular tool for visualizing procurement schedules. They help map out each procurement activity, its duration, and its dependencies on other tasks. This allows project managers to identify potential bottlenecks and allocate resources effectively.

Procurement Scheduling Tools
Project management software such as Microsoft Project, Primavera, or specialized procurement tools like SAP Ariba can automate scheduling tasks. These tools allow for:

> Setting deadlines for issuing purchase orders and receiving deliveries.

> Monitoring progress in real time.

> Adjusting schedules dynamically to address unforeseen changes.

Budgeting and Cost Estimation
Budgeting tools play a crucial role in controlling procurement costs. Techniques such as zero-based budgeting or cost estimation models can help in creating realistic financial plans.

Total Cost of Ownership (TCO)
TCO is a valuable metric for budgeting. It considers not only the purchase price but also additional costs such as transportation, maintenance, and disposal. For example, a lower-priced machine may incur higher maintenance costs, making it less cost-effective in the long run.

Cost Management Software
Software tools like Oracle NetSuite or QuickBooks enable organizations to track procurement expenditures, compare them against budgets, and identify cost-saving opportunities.

Common Pitfalls in Procurement Planning

Despite its importance, procurement planning is susceptible to challenges that can derail project success. Understanding and avoiding these pitfalls is crucial.

Inadequate Needs Assessment
Failing to conduct a thorough needs assessment can lead to procuring unnecessary items or overlooking critical ones. This often results in wasted resources or project delays.

Unrealistic Timelines
Overly optimistic scheduling can create pressure on suppliers and procurement teams, increasing the likelihood of errors and missed deadlines. It's essential to account for contingencies and supplier lead times when planning.

Budget Overruns
Underestimating costs or neglecting hidden expenses can lead to budget overruns. For instance, shipping and customs fees for international procurement may not be accounted for, straining project finances.

Supplier Misalignment
Selecting suppliers without aligning their capabilities with project requirements can result in poor-quality deliverables or delays. Proper prequalification and evaluation of suppliers are essential.

Inefficient Communication
Lack of clear communication between procurement teams, suppliers, and stakeholders can cause misunderstandings and errors. Establishing

regular communication channels and using collaboration tools can mitigate this risk.

Failure to Monitor and Adapt
Procurement plans must be dynamic and adaptable to changes. Rigid plans that fail to address evolving project needs or market conditions can hinder success.

Procurement planning is the cornerstone of successful project execution. By creating a comprehensive procurement management plan, leveraging tools for scheduling and budgeting, and avoiding common pitfalls, organizations can ensure that procurement activities align with project goals. Thoughtful planning reduces risks, optimizes resources, and sets the stage for seamless procurement execution, ultimately contributing to the overall success of the project.

7. Market Analysis and Supplier Research

Market analysis and supplier research are foundational elements of procurement that directly influence project outcomes. By understanding the market landscape and identifying suitable suppliers, organizations can make informed decisions that balance cost, quality, and timelines. Additionally, staying abreast of industry trends empowers procurement teams to adopt innovative practices, remain competitive, and mitigate risks. This chapter delves into the processes and tools for conducting market assessments, identifying potential suppliers, and analyzing industry trends to enhance procurement strategies.

Conducting Market Assessments

A market assessment is a systematic process of analyzing the external environment to identify opportunities, threats, and dynamics that could impact procurement decisions. It provides insights into supplier availability, pricing trends, and market competitiveness.

Understanding the Market Landscape
To conduct a thorough market assessment, it is crucial to understand the following elements:

> **Market Size and Segmentation**: Identifying the scale of the market and its key segments helps procurement teams focus on areas most relevant to their needs. For example, in the technology sector, segmentation might include hardware suppliers, software vendors, and cloud service providers.

> **Market Dynamics**: Analyzing supply-demand trends, price fluctuations, and regulatory changes allows organizations to anticipate challenges and adapt accordingly.

Data Collection and Analysis
Gathering accurate data is essential for market assessments. This can be achieved through:

Primary Research: Engaging directly with suppliers, conducting surveys, and attending trade fairs provide firsthand information.

Secondary Research: Leveraging industry reports, government publications, and online databases offers a broader perspective on market conditions.

Competitor Analysis: Studying how competitors source materials or services can reveal valuable insights and benchmarks.

SWOT Analysis in Procurement

Using SWOT analysis—identifying strengths, weaknesses, opportunities, and threats—enables organizations to evaluate the viability of sourcing strategies within the market context. For instance, recognizing a supplier's strong distribution network as a strength while identifying potential delays in raw material availability as a threat can inform contingency planning.

Identifying Potential Suppliers

Selecting the right suppliers is a critical step that influences quality, cost, and project timelines. The process of identifying potential suppliers involves systematic research and evaluation.

Sources for Supplier Identification

Online Directories: Platforms such as ThomasNet, Alibaba, and Kompass allow procurement teams to access a wide range of supplier information.

Industry Networks and Associations: Professional organizations and industry groups often provide recommendations for reliable suppliers.

Referrals and Recommendations: Leveraging recommendations from trusted partners or stakeholders can help identify vetted suppliers.

Trade Shows and Conferences: Participating in industry events offers an opportunity to meet potential suppliers, view product samples, and establish connections.

Criteria for Supplier Selection
Identifying potential suppliers requires evaluating them against predetermined criteria, including:

Capabilities and Capacity: Assess whether the supplier can meet the project's technical requirements and volume demands.

Financial Stability: Verify the supplier's financial health to ensure long-term reliability.

Reputation and Track Record: Review past performance, customer testimonials, and any awards or certifications.

Geographical Proximity: For certain projects, proximity can reduce shipping costs and lead times.

Prequalification and Longlisting
Once potential suppliers are identified, a prequalification process ensures that only those meeting minimum standards proceed to the next stage. A longlist of qualified suppliers is created based on preliminary evaluations, which is then narrowed down during the request for proposal (RFP) or tendering process.

Analyzing Industry Trends for Better Procurement Decisions

Staying informed about industry trends allows procurement teams to anticipate changes, adopt innovations, and mitigate risks effectively.

Emerging Technologies

Advances in technology often reshape procurement practices. For instance:

>**Artificial Intelligence (AI)**: AI-powered tools enable predictive analytics, helping organizations forecast demand and optimize supplier selection.
>
>**Blockchain**: Blockchain enhances transparency and traceability in supply chains, reducing fraud and improving trust with suppliers.

Sustainability and Green Procurement

Increasing emphasis on sustainability is influencing procurement strategies across industries. Organizations are prioritizing suppliers that:

>Offer eco-friendly products or services.
>
>Adhere to environmental regulations.
>
>Incorporate circular economy principles, such as recycling and reuse.

Globalization and Supply Chain Risks

Global sourcing is expanding access to competitive pricing and diverse suppliers but also introduces risks such as geopolitical instability and supply chain disruptions. Analyzing trends in global trade, tariffs, and customs regulations is essential for minimizing such risks.

Market Consolidation

In some industries, supplier markets are consolidating, with fewer large players dominating. This can impact pricing power and supplier availability. Understanding such trends helps procurement teams develop strategies to negotiate favorable terms or explore alternative sources.

Tools for Trend Analysis
Procurement teams can leverage tools and techniques for monitoring industry trends:

Porter's Five Forces: This framework assesses competitive forces, including supplier power and market competition, to understand market dynamics.

Scenario Planning: Developing scenarios for potential market developments allows teams to prepare for a range of outcomes.

Market Intelligence Platforms: Tools like Gartner, IBISWorld, and ProcurementIQ provide access to up-to-date market analysis.

Integrating Insights into Procurement Strategies
Insights from market and trend analyses should be integrated into procurement planning and decision-making. For example, identifying a shift toward automation in manufacturing could prompt an organization to prioritize suppliers who offer technologically advanced solutions.

Market analysis and supplier research are indispensable components of procurement planning. By conducting thorough market assessments, identifying potential suppliers, and analyzing industry trends, organizations can make informed procurement decisions that align with project goals. This proactive approach ensures access to reliable suppliers, competitive pricing, and innovative practices, ultimately driving project success.

8. Supplier Prequalification and Evaluation

Supplier prequalification and evaluation are integral to the procurement process, ensuring that only suppliers capable of meeting the project's requirements proceed through the sourcing stages. Prequalification helps organizations reduce risk, improve procurement efficiency, and foster long-term supplier relationships. This chapter explores the process of establishing prequalification criteria, conducting supplier audits, and utilizing various tools and techniques to evaluate potential suppliers effectively.

Establishing Prequalification Criteria

The prequalification process begins by establishing clear and comprehensive criteria to evaluate the capabilities of potential suppliers. This ensures that only those who meet the minimum requirements are considered, saving time and effort later in the procurement process. Prequalification criteria typically focus on several key factors, including financial stability, technical expertise, experience, and compliance with regulatory requirements.

Key Elements of Prequalification Criteria

Financial Stability: A supplier's financial health is critical for ensuring they can fulfill orders on time and handle unforeseen challenges. This can be assessed by reviewing financial statements, credit scores, and payment history. A financially stable supplier is more likely to remain reliable throughout the contract term.

Experience and Track Record: The supplier's experience in the relevant industry or with similar projects is a key indicator of their ability to deliver. Analyzing past projects, client feedback, and performance evaluations will provide insight into their reliability and quality of work.

Technical Capabilities: Suppliers should possess the technical skills and infrastructure needed to meet project specifications. Prequalification often includes assessing the supplier's equipment, production capacity, and ability to innovate or adapt to changing needs.

Regulatory Compliance: Ensuring that potential suppliers comply with relevant legal, environmental, and industry-specific regulations is a vital aspect of prequalification. This includes compliance with health and safety standards, environmental regulations, labor laws, and any other applicable industry certifications.

Quality Assurance: Suppliers must demonstrate a commitment to quality control and continuous improvement. The use of international standards such as ISO certifications can be an indicator of their quality management systems.

Delivery and Logistics Capabilities: Suppliers should be evaluated on their ability to meet project timelines, handle logistics, and manage supply chains effectively. This includes assessing their transportation networks, distribution facilities, and capacity for scaling operations if necessary.

Ethical Standards and Corporate Social Responsibility (CSR): Prequalification should also examine the supplier's commitment to ethical business practices, such as anti-corruption policies, labor rights, sustainability initiatives, and community engagement.

Prequalification Process

Issuing a Supplier Questionnaire: The first step in the prequalification process often involves sending potential suppliers a detailed questionnaire. This helps gather data about their financial health, capabilities, and compliance with regulatory standards.

Document Review and Assessment: Suppliers' submitted documents (such as financial statements, certifications, and proof of past performance) are carefully reviewed to ensure they meet the predefined criteria.

Site Visits and Interviews: Depending on the complexity of the project and the supplier's location, site visits and interviews may be necessary. These visits allow for a firsthand assessment of the supplier's facilities, processes, and operational capabilities.

Supplier Shortlisting: After evaluating suppliers based on the prequalification criteria, a shortlist is created. Suppliers that do not meet the criteria are removed from consideration, while those who qualify are invited to submit bids or participate in further evaluations.

Conducting Supplier Audits

Supplier audits are a critical step in verifying that the supplier operates according to agreed standards and processes. Audits provide a detailed, objective assessment of a supplier's operations, helping procurement teams identify potential risks, improve quality, and ensure compliance. Supplier audits can be both proactive, as part of the initial prequalification, and ongoing, as part of continuous supplier management.

Types of Supplier Audits

Financial Audits: These audits assess the financial health of a supplier, ensuring that they are financially sound and capable of fulfilling long-term contracts. They involve reviewing financial statements, profit and loss accounts, tax records, and credit reports.

Quality Audits: Quality audits evaluate the supplier's adherence to quality standards. These audits assess manufacturing processes, product quality control measures, testing protocols, and inspection procedures. Suppliers are often required to comply with ISO 9001 or similar quality certifications.

Environmental Audits: These audits focus on the environmental impact of the supplier's operations, including waste management, resource consumption, pollution control measures, and adherence to environmental regulations.

Compliance Audits: Compliance audits examine whether the supplier adheres to regulatory requirements in areas such as labor laws, health and safety standards, and ethical practices. Suppliers may be audited for compliance with specific standards, such as ISO 14001 for environmental management or SA8000 for social accountability.

Process Audits: These audits assess the supplier's operational processes, including procurement, production, logistics, and delivery. They help identify inefficiencies and opportunities for improvement in the supplier's workflow.

Conducting an Effective Supplier Audit

Pre-Audit Preparation: Before conducting an audit, it is essential to establish the scope, objectives, and criteria for evaluation. This may involve reviewing the supplier's previous audit reports and defining key areas of focus.

On-Site Audit: On-site audits involve visiting the supplier's facilities to conduct assessments in person. This may include inspecting production lines, meeting with management, and reviewing documentation.

Interviews and Observations: Conducting interviews with key personnel and observing operational practices provides additional context to the audit process. This can help identify potential issues related to management, employee training, or system inefficiencies.

Audit Reporting: After the audit, a comprehensive report is generated, outlining the findings, strengths, weaknesses, and any recommendations for improvement. This report helps the procurement team make data-driven decisions about whether to continue working with the supplier.

Tools and Techniques for Supplier Evaluation

Effective supplier evaluation involves using structured tools and techniques to assess suppliers against pre-established criteria. Various methods help procurement teams assess supplier performance, compare options, and make informed decisions.

Supplier Evaluation Tools

Supplier Scorecards: A supplier scorecard is a comprehensive tool used to evaluate and track supplier performance over time. It typically includes metrics related to quality, delivery, price, service, and compliance. A weighted scoring system allows procurement teams to compare suppliers based on their overall performance.

360-Degree Feedback: This technique involves collecting feedback from multiple sources, including internal stakeholders, quality control teams, and external customers. It provides a well-rounded view of a supplier's performance and capabilities.

Key Performance Indicators (KPIs): KPIs are specific metrics used to assess the supplier's performance. Common KPIs include on-time delivery rate, defect rate, and order fulfillment accuracy.

Supplier Performance Reviews: Regular performance reviews help assess how well suppliers meet their contractual obligations. These reviews typically involve meetings between procurement teams and suppliers to discuss past performance, identify issues, and set improvement targets.

Benchmarking: Benchmarking involves comparing a supplier's performance to industry standards or the performance of other suppliers. This technique helps identify areas for improvement and ensures that the supplier remains competitive in the market.

Evaluation Techniques

Cost-Benefit Analysis: This technique compares the costs of working with a supplier to the benefits they provide. Factors such as pricing, delivery terms, and quality are weighed against the supplier's reliability and long-term value.

Multi-Criteria Decision Analysis (MCDA): MCDA involves evaluating suppliers across several criteria, each with a weight based on its importance. The total score helps determine which supplier is the best fit for the project.

Risk Assessment: A supplier evaluation should also include a risk assessment to identify potential risks such as financial instability, supply chain disruptions, and non-compliance with regulations. This helps mitigate potential issues before they impact the project.

Supplier prequalification and evaluation are essential components of a robust procurement process. By establishing clear prequalification criteria, conducting thorough supplier audits, and leveraging evaluation tools, organizations can ensure they select the right suppliers to meet their project needs. These processes help mitigate risks, ensure compliance, and promote long-term supplier relationships, ultimately contributing to the success of the project.

9. Request for Proposals (RFP) and Tendering Processes

The Request for Proposal (RFP) and tendering processes are essential tools in procurement, enabling organizations to acquire goods and services that meet their specific needs. A well-designed RFP and a structured tendering process ensure transparency, competitive pricing, and the selection of the best supplier for a project. This chapter delves into the intricacies of designing clear and comprehensive RFPs, managing the tendering process, and evaluating bids using weighted criteria.

Designing Clear and Comprehensive RFPs

A Request for Proposal (RFP) is a formal document issued by an organization to solicit proposals from suppliers or service providers. It outlines the organization's needs, expectations, and requirements for a particular project or service. Designing an effective RFP is essential to ensuring that vendors understand the project scope, objectives, and terms, allowing them to submit competitive and relevant bids.

Key Components of an RFP

Introduction and Background: The introduction provides an overview of the organization issuing the RFP and the background information related to the project. It sets the context for why the RFP has been issued and outlines the goals and objectives of the procurement process.

Project Scope and Requirements: The most crucial section of the RFP, the scope and requirements, details what the organization needs. This includes specific deliverables, performance standards, timelines, and the expected outcomes of the project. A clear definition of the project scope ensures that suppliers submit proposals that meet the actual needs of the organization.

Evaluation Criteria: This section outlines how the proposals will be evaluated. The evaluation criteria can include factors such as cost, technical expertise, quality, experience, and timelines. Providing these criteria upfront helps suppliers tailor their proposals to meet the organization's expectations.

Proposal Submission Guidelines: The RFP should include clear instructions on how vendors should submit their proposals. This can include formatting requirements, the submission deadline, and the method of submission (e.g., electronic submission or physical copies).

Terms and Conditions: The terms and conditions section should outline the legal and contractual obligations that will govern the relationship between the buyer and the supplier. This includes payment terms, intellectual property rights, confidentiality agreements, and dispute resolution mechanisms.

Questions and Clarifications: Often, suppliers may have questions or need clarification about the RFP's requirements. A section should be dedicated to addressing these inquiries, along with a designated timeline for submission.

Best Practices for Designing an RFP

Be Specific and Detailed: A well-written RFP eliminates ambiguity. The more specific the requirements, the more accurate the proposals will be. Providing clear definitions of deliverables, deadlines, and performance standards ensures suppliers understand what is expected.

Align with Strategic Objectives: Ensure that the RFP aligns with the organization's overall strategic goals. This ensures that the selected supplier will contribute to long-term success.

Engage Stakeholders Early: Involve internal stakeholders from different departments during the RFP design process to ensure that all requirements are captured. This collaborative approach helps prevent gaps in the RFP and ensures comprehensive coverage.

Maintain Clarity and Consistency: The language in the RFP should be clear, concise, and consistent throughout. Avoid jargon or complex terminology that could confuse potential suppliers.

Offer Support and Resources: Provide vendors with the necessary information, such as templates, guidelines, or frequently asked questions, to assist them in preparing their proposals.

Managing the Tendering Process

The tendering process is the method by which an organization solicits, receives, and evaluates bids or proposals. It is a critical aspect of procurement, ensuring that the organization selects the right supplier while adhering to legal, regulatory, and ethical standards. Managing the tendering process effectively is essential for achieving the best value for money and ensuring that the procurement process is fair and transparent.

Steps in the Tendering Process

Issuing the RFP: The first step in the tendering process is issuing the RFP to potential suppliers. This may be done through various channels, including industry networks, online portals, or direct invitations to prequalified vendors.

Bidder Clarifications: After the RFP is issued, suppliers may seek clarification on the requirements. It is important to establish a formal process for responding to questions and distributing answers to all potential bidders to maintain fairness.

Receiving Bids: Suppliers submit their bids or proposals by the specified deadline. It is essential to ensure that bids are submitted according to the guidelines in the RFP and that the submission process is secure and confidential.

Opening the Bids: Bid opening should be conducted transparently, ideally in the presence of representatives from both parties or external observers. A formal bid opening ensures that all bids are reviewed fairly and that no supplier has an unfair advantage.

Bid Evaluation: This step involves evaluating the bids based on the pre-established criteria. Evaluators should have a clear understanding of the selection process and ensure that all bids are considered objectively and consistently.

Negotiation and Awarding the Contract: After evaluating the bids, the selected supplier is invited to negotiate terms, if necessary, before a final decision is made. Once negotiations are complete, the contract is awarded to the winning supplier.

Feedback to Unsuccessful Bidders: After the contract is awarded, it is best practice to provide feedback to unsuccessful bidders. This helps build good relationships with vendors and encourages them to submit better proposals in the future.

Best Practices for Managing the Tendering Process

Establish Clear Deadlines: Setting clear deadlines for bid submission, questions, and evaluations ensures that the tendering process runs smoothly and on schedule.

Ensure Transparency: Transparency throughout the tendering process fosters trust among suppliers and prevents potential disputes. All suppliers should have access to the same information and be evaluated according to the same criteria.

Maintain Confidentiality: It is crucial to maintain confidentiality throughout the process. This includes safeguarding proprietary information in the bids and ensuring that evaluation decisions are not influenced by external factors.

Use a Structured Evaluation Process: Use a structured evaluation process that is documented and repeatable. This helps ensure that every bid is evaluated on the same basis and reduces the risk of bias or favoritism.

Evaluating Bids Using Weighted Criteria

Evaluating bids is one of the most crucial aspects of the procurement process. To ensure that suppliers are assessed fairly, organizations often use a weighted scoring system that takes into account various criteria important for the project's success. Weighted criteria allow decision-makers to compare bids objectively, accounting for both quantitative and qualitative factors.

Steps in Bid Evaluation

Define Evaluation Criteria: The first step in bid evaluation is defining the criteria by which bids will be assessed. This includes both mandatory criteria (e.g., legal compliance, technical capability) and desirable criteria (e.g., experience, pricing).

Assign Weights to Criteria: Once the evaluation criteria are defined, weights are assigned based on their relative importance to the success of the project. For example, price may account for 40% of the total score, while technical expertise may account for 30%, and delivery time for 20%.

Evaluate Each Bid: Bids are then evaluated based on how well they meet each criterion. For each bid, a score is assigned for each criterion, with the score reflecting the extent to which the bid meets the requirement.

Multiply Scores by Weights: The scores for each criterion are multiplied by the corresponding weight to calculate a weighted score. This ensures that the most important factors have a greater impact on the final evaluation.

Summing Weighted Scores: Once all the scores are multiplied by their respective weights, the weighted scores are summed to produce an overall score for each bid.

Selecting the Winning Bid: The bid with the highest overall score is typically selected as the winner, though other factors such as negotiation outcomes and strategic alignment may also influence the decision.

Best Practices for Bid Evaluation

Develop a Standardized Scoring System: Ensure that the scoring system is standardized so that all bids are evaluated consistently.

Involve Multiple Evaluators: Involving multiple evaluators in the bid evaluation process helps reduce bias and ensures a balanced decision-making process.

Document the Evaluation Process: Documenting the evaluation process and the rationale for selecting the winning bid helps maintain transparency and provides a reference in case of disputes.

Consider Long-Term Value: While price is an important factor, it should not be the only consideration. Long-term value, including quality, reliability, and the supplier's ability to meet future needs, should also be factored into the evaluation.

The RFP and tendering processes play a vital role in ensuring the procurement of high-quality goods and services that meet the organization's objectives. By designing clear and comprehensive RFPs, managing the tendering process efficiently, and using weighted criteria to evaluate bids, organizations can make informed decisions, reduce risks, and achieve the best value for money. Effective implementation of these processes fosters strong supplier relationships and contributes to the success of the overall project.

10.Vendor Relationships and Collaboration

In today's highly competitive business environment, the relationship between a company and its suppliers is crucial to the success of any project. Procurement is no longer seen as a transactional process but as a strategic partnership that adds value to both parties involved. Building long-term, mutually beneficial relationships with vendors and suppliers, managing strategic alliances, and handling difficult suppliers effectively are all integral to achieving sustainable project success. This chapter explores these critical aspects of vendor management, providing detailed insights and practical approaches for managing supplier relationships in a professional and efficient manner.

Building Long-Term Supplier Partnerships

Building long-term supplier partnerships is an essential part of modern procurement strategies. When businesses collaborate closely with their suppliers over extended periods, both sides benefit from shared knowledge, continuous improvement, and a stable, predictable supply chain. Long-term relationships reduce risks associated with procurement, such as price volatility and supply chain disruptions, and help foster innovation.

One of the primary benefits of long-term supplier relationships is the alignment of objectives. When suppliers are seen as partners rather than mere service providers, they are more likely to understand the company's strategic goals and contribute to achieving them. This alignment can lead to joint problem-solving, co-innovation, and the ability to respond more effectively to market changes or challenges.

Key Strategies for Building Long-Term Partnerships

Clear Communication: Communication is at the heart of any successful partnership. Regular meetings, updates, and open dialogue help build trust and understanding. It's crucial for businesses to communicate their needs, concerns, and expectations clearly, while also listening to their suppliers. Transparent communication regarding issues such as delivery schedules, changes in requirements, and pricing adjustments ensures that both parties can plan accordingly.

Shared Risk and Reward: In a true partnership, both parties share the risks and rewards. Suppliers that are deeply embedded in a company's supply chain should not only benefit from steady, reliable business but also share in the risks associated with fluctuations in demand or supply chain disruptions. This can be formalized through joint performance metrics or incentive programs that reward suppliers for achieving key targets such as quality standards, on-time delivery, or cost reduction.

Investment in Supplier Development: Building long-term relationships requires mutual investment. Companies that are serious about fostering strong vendor relationships should invest in their suppliers' capabilities. This could involve providing suppliers with access to training, technology, or resources to help improve their performance. This investment fosters loyalty and strengthens the overall supply chain by ensuring that suppliers have the necessary tools to meet expectations.

Consistent Performance Evaluation and Feedback: Long-term supplier relationships require ongoing assessment and improvement. Regular performance evaluations provide both parties with a clear understanding of where they stand in terms of meeting their objectives. Providing feedback on areas of improvement is critical, as it enables suppliers to make adjustments and improve their service over time. Supplier evaluations should not only focus on metrics like cost and delivery times but should also include aspects like quality, flexibility, and innovation.

Managing Strategic Alliances for Projects

Strategic alliances involve collaborating with suppliers who offer critical resources or capabilities that complement the buyer's own capabilities. In project procurement, strategic alliances can enhance the project's overall value by leveraging the strengths of key partners and sharing responsibilities for project success.

What Makes a Strategic Alliance Successful?
A successful strategic alliance goes beyond the simple exchange of goods and services; it is a collaborative relationship in which both parties invest in each other's success. Successful strategic alliances in project procurement require the following elements:

> **Alignment of Goals and Objectives**: For an alliance to succeed, both parties need to have aligned strategic goals. This means that each party should understand the objectives of the other and how the alliance contributes to achieving those goals. For example, a supplier may be more willing to prioritize your project if they understand how it fits into their long-term objectives, such as growth, market positioning, or innovation.

> **Mutual Trust and Respect**: Trust is fundamental in any alliance. Both partners need to believe that the other will act in good faith and work toward mutual success. Trust is built through consistent actions, open communication, and fulfilling commitments. This respect is crucial when it comes to negotiating and making decisions together during the course of the project.

> **Joint Investment in Resources and Capabilities**: Strategic alliances often involve significant resource sharing, such as technology, knowledge, and finances. Each party must be willing to invest in the partnership to ensure its success. For instance, a company may share its proprietary process technology with a supplier, or a supplier may invest in the infrastructure needed to fulfill an order more efficiently.

Innovation and Knowledge Sharing: One of the most significant advantages of strategic alliances is the ability to co-develop new solutions. By pooling knowledge and expertise, both parties can create innovations that would not be possible individually. Strategic alliances can serve as a platform for suppliers and customers to jointly solve problems, improve products, or reduce costs.

Risk Sharing: Alliances work best when both parties share the risks of the project. This could mean providing financial backing for R&D, jointly investing in new manufacturing processes, or sharing the financial consequences of project delays. By distributing risks, both companies are more likely to stay committed to the success of the project and work together to mitigate problems as they arise.

Key Challenges in Managing Strategic Alliances

While strategic alliances offer numerous benefits, they also present unique challenges. One of the primary challenges is ensuring alignment of goals and interests throughout the duration of the project. Over time, business priorities may change, and what was once a mutually beneficial relationship may become strained. This can be particularly difficult if there is an imbalance of power between the partners or if one party begins to feel that they are contributing more than the other. To avoid these issues, it is important to define clear governance structures, performance metrics, and regular review cycles.

Another challenge is managing cultural differences, especially in global alliances. Different working styles, communication approaches, and business practices can cause friction between partners. Establishing clear communication protocols, regular meetings, and a culture of mutual respect can help mitigate these challenges.

Dealing with Difficult Suppliers

Despite efforts to build positive relationships with vendors, challenges will inevitably arise, and not all supplier relationships will be smooth. Whether dealing with underperformance, disputes, or communication issues, effective supplier management is essential to ensuring that a project continues to move forward successfully.

Identifying the Root Causes of Supplier Issues

To effectively deal with difficult suppliers, it is essential first to understand the root cause of the issue. Problems could arise from a variety of factors, including:

Poor Communication: Misunderstandings or miscommunications often lead to conflicts with suppliers. If a supplier is not clear on expectations, timelines, or quality requirements, it can result in mistakes, delays, or dissatisfaction.

Lack of Capacity or Capability: Sometimes, a supplier may struggle to meet your project's requirements due to limitations in their capacity, technology, or expertise. Identifying these constraints early on can help manage expectations and provide a path for addressing these gaps.

Cultural and Organizational Differences: Differences in business culture, management style, or operational practices can create tension between a company and its suppliers. These differences often become apparent when problems arise, and without addressing them, they can escalate into significant disputes.

Unforeseen External Factors: External factors such as market changes, economic conditions, or political instability can impact a supplier's ability to deliver as promised. While these are often outside of the supplier's control, it is important to have contingency plans in place to minimize the impact on the project.

Effective Approaches for Dealing with Difficult Suppliers

Open and Honest Communication: When issues arise, open and honest communication is key. It's important to approach difficult suppliers with a mindset of collaboration rather than confrontation.

Instead of blaming, focus on understanding the issue and finding a solution together. Regular meetings, performance reviews, and discussions about progress can prevent small issues from growing into larger problems.

Escalation Procedures: When problems cannot be resolved at the operational level, it may be necessary to escalate the issue. Having a clear escalation procedure ensures that problems are addressed at the appropriate level of the organization and that all parties understand the process.

Re-negotiating Terms and Expectations: In cases where a supplier cannot meet agreed-upon terms, renegotiating terms or extending timelines may be necessary. If the supplier's inability to deliver is due to unforeseen challenges, working together to find a mutually acceptable solution can help maintain a productive relationship.

Seek Mediation: If conflicts persist and are affecting the project's success, bringing in a third-party mediator can help resolve disputes without escalating them to legal action. Mediation provides both parties with an opportunity to present their case and negotiate a fair solution.

Termination of the Relationship: In cases where the relationship cannot be salvaged, and the supplier is unable or unwilling to meet the project's needs, it may be necessary to end the partnership. However, this should be a last resort after all other avenues have been exhausted.

Vendor relationships and collaboration are central to the success of any project. Whether building long-term supplier partnerships, managing strategic alliances, or dealing with difficult suppliers, the way companies engage with their vendors can significantly impact the outcomes of their projects. Strong relationships based on clear communication, shared goals, and mutual respect lead to more successful collaborations, while effective supplier management strategies can help resolve conflicts and ensure that projects stay on track. By focusing on building positive, productive relationships with suppliers, organizations can ensure that their procurement processes contribute to their overall strategic goals.

Section 3: Contracting and Negotiations

11. Contract Types and Selection

Effective contracting and negotiation are central to successful project procurement. The type of contract selected has a significant impact on project delivery, cost control, and the overall relationship between the buyer and supplier. The right contract ensures clear expectations, defines the scope of work, and allocates risks appropriately between the parties involved. This chapter delves into the various types of contracts, their selection criteria, and when to use innovative contracting models to optimize project outcomes.

Fixed-Price vs. Cost-Plus Contracts

Two of the most commonly used contract types in project procurement are fixed-price and cost-plus contracts. Each offers different advantages and is suitable for different types of projects. Understanding these contract types helps project managers make informed decisions and reduce risks.

Fixed-Price Contracts

A fixed-price contract (also known as a lump-sum contract) is an agreement where the buyer and seller agree on a fixed price for the entire scope of work. The price is agreed upon before the work begins and does not change, regardless of the actual costs incurred by the supplier during the execution of the project. This type of contract provides clear cost expectations for both parties and is often used when the project's scope, timeline, and deliverables are well-defined.

Advantages of Fixed-Price Contracts

> **Cost Certainty**: The buyer knows the cost upfront, which helps in budgeting and forecasting. This certainty is particularly important for projects with limited financial resources or those that need to stay within a fixed budget.

Clear Deliverables: Fixed-price contracts are ideal when the project scope is well-defined, as it allows the buyer to clearly outline the deliverables and timelines.

Incentivized Performance: Suppliers have a clear incentive to control costs and complete the project efficiently, as any cost savings are retained as profit. This can lead to greater project efficiency and innovation.

Disadvantages of Fixed-Price Contracts

Limited Flexibility: Fixed-price contracts may lack flexibility if there are changes in the scope, schedule, or specifications. Any modification typically requires renegotiation of the contract terms.

Higher Risk for Suppliers: The supplier assumes most of the risk, particularly if costs exceed the fixed price due to unforeseen circumstances. This can result in cost-cutting measures that affect quality.

Potential for Misaligned Interests: Suppliers may focus on reducing costs at the expense of quality or other factors important to the buyer, leading to potential performance issues.

When to Use Fixed-Price Contracts

Fixed-price contracts are best suited for projects with well-defined scopes, specifications, and timelines. These contracts are ideal when the project requirements are unlikely to change significantly, such as in construction projects, product development, or any project where the buyer and seller can accurately estimate the cost and schedule. Fixed-price contracts also work well when a competitive bidding process is involved, as suppliers may compete based on their ability to offer the best price.

Cost-Plus Contracts

In a cost-plus contract, the buyer agrees to reimburse the supplier for the actual costs incurred during the project, including labor, materials, and overheads, plus an additional amount for profit (a percentage of the total costs or a fixed fee). Unlike fixed-price contracts, cost-plus contracts do not set a firm price upfront but provide a more flexible arrangement that accommodates changes in scope or unforeseen conditions.

Advantages of Cost-Plus Contracts

Flexibility: Cost-plus contracts offer greater flexibility, allowing for adjustments to the scope, schedule, or specifications without the need for extensive renegotiation.

Reduced Risk for Suppliers: Since the buyer assumes most of the financial risk in a cost-plus arrangement, suppliers are more likely to be willing to take on projects with uncertain scopes or complex requirements.

Encourages High-Quality Work: With a cost-plus contract, suppliers may feel incentivized to perform high-quality work, as they are reimbursed for the actual costs incurred, which can reduce the temptation to cut corners.

Disadvantages of Cost-Plus Contracts

Uncertainty of Final Costs: The primary drawback of a cost-plus contract is the uncertainty of the total project cost. This can make budgeting and cost control challenging for the buyer.

Lack of Incentive to Control Costs: Unlike fixed-price contracts, cost-plus agreements may not incentivize suppliers to minimize costs, as they are reimbursed for expenses. This can lead to inefficiencies, budget overruns, or unnecessary expenses.

Complex Monitoring and Administration: Cost-plus contracts require detailed tracking of costs, receipts, and expenses, which can be time-consuming and require more extensive oversight from both parties.

When to Use Cost-Plus Contracts

Cost-plus contracts are ideal for projects where the scope is uncertain, complex, or likely to change over time. These contracts are often used in research and development, software development, or any project with a high degree of uncertainty or innovation. Cost-plus arrangements are also useful when the buyer wants to encourage suppliers to explore creative solutions and does not want to stifle innovation by limiting the budget.

When to Use Time and Material Contracts

Time and material contracts (T&M) are another common type of agreement used in project procurement. In a T&M contract, the buyer agrees to pay the supplier based on the actual time spent working (usually billed at an hourly or daily rate) and the materials used in the project. This type of contract is used when the exact scope of work is not clearly defined, and both parties agree that the project will evolve over time.

Advantages of Time and Material Contracts

Flexibility: T&M contracts allow for significant flexibility as both the scope and schedule are adaptable to changes. This is particularly useful in projects with evolving requirements or uncertain timelines.

Transparency: The buyer can track the supplier's actual time and material usage, which promotes transparency in the relationship.

Faster Procurement: T&M contracts can be easier to establish quickly when the scope is not fully defined, as they do not require extensive upfront planning or estimation.

Disadvantages of Time and Material Contracts

Uncertainty in Costs: Since the final cost is based on the actual time and materials used, there is significant uncertainty around the total project cost.

Risk of Scope Creep: Without clear project boundaries, there is a risk of scope creep, where the project expands beyond its original scope, leading to higher costs and extended timelines.

Lack of Cost Control Incentive: Suppliers may have little incentive to complete the work quickly or cost-effectively, as they are paid based on the time and materials used.

When to Use Time and Material Contracts

T&M contracts are suitable for projects with uncertain scopes, where the exact work to be done is not easily defined, or when work is expected to be ongoing over an extended period. They are often used in maintenance contracts, IT services, consulting, or projects with continuous changes or exploratory work. T&M contracts are also common when the buyer needs a supplier to perform tasks that are difficult to quantify, such as repairs or troubleshooting.

Innovative Contracting Models

As industries evolve and project requirements become more complex, traditional contracting models may no longer provide the best solutions. In response, organizations are increasingly adopting innovative contracting models to improve performance, manage risks, and foster better relationships with suppliers.

Performance-Based Contracts

A performance-based contract focuses on the delivery of specific outcomes or results rather than the inputs (such as hours worked or materials used). In this model, the buyer and supplier agree on key performance indicators (KPIs) or measurable deliverables that the supplier must meet to receive payment. Performance-based contracts are especially useful in projects where the quality of the output is more important than the specific methods or processes used by the supplier.

Advantages

Alignment of Interests: Both parties are aligned in their desire to meet performance goals, fostering collaboration.

Improved Quality: Since payment is tied to the achievement of specific results, suppliers are incentivized to produce high-quality outcomes.

Disadvantages

Difficulty in Defining Metrics: It can be challenging to define clear, measurable performance metrics, especially in projects with intangible or subjective deliverables.

Risk of Disputes: If the performance criteria are not clearly defined, there may be disputes over whether the supplier has met the requirements.

Collaborative Contracts

Collaborative contracts focus on creating a strong, long-term relationship between the buyer and supplier, with both parties working together to achieve mutual goals. These contracts often involve shared risks, rewards, and responsibilities and are based on cooperation rather than competition. They are particularly effective in complex projects where both parties need to invest time and resources to ensure success.

Advantages

Risk Sharing: Both parties share the risks and rewards, creating a sense of partnership.

Innovation and Problem Solving: A collaborative approach can lead to innovative solutions and more effective problem-solving.

Disadvantages

Complexity: Collaborative contracts require a high degree of trust and communication, which can make them difficult to manage.

Long-Term Commitment: These contracts are best suited for long-term, ongoing relationships, which may not be feasible for all projects.

Selecting the appropriate contract type is crucial to the success of any project. Whether opting for a fixed-price contract to ensure cost certainty, a cost-plus contract to accommodate uncertainty, or a time and material contract to handle evolving requirements, each contract type has distinct advantages and disadvantages. Innovative contracting models, such as performance-based and collaborative contracts, are becoming increasingly popular for projects that require flexibility, performance incentives, and strong supplier relationships. By understanding the strengths and weaknesses of different contract types, project managers can make more informed decisions that align with the project's goals and ensure successful outcomes.

12.Contract Drafting and Review

Effective contract drafting and review are crucial components in ensuring the success of a project. Well-drafted contracts set clear expectations, mitigate risks, and establish a legal framework that helps resolve disputes if they arise. This chapter will explore the key clauses in project contracts, provide strategies for ensuring fairness and transparency in agreements, and discuss how to handle intellectual property (IP) and confidentiality issues.

Key Clauses in Project Contracts

A project contract consists of various clauses that define the terms and conditions under which the parties agree to execute the work. These clauses are fundamental for setting clear expectations and protecting the interests of both the buyer and the supplier. Below are the most critical clauses typically found in project contracts:

Scope of Work
The scope of work (SOW) is the heart of the contract. It clearly outlines the project's deliverables, milestones, timelines, and specifications. It defines what will and will not be included in the project, ensuring that both parties have a mutual understanding of the project's objectives. A comprehensive SOW helps prevent scope creep, where additional tasks or changes are introduced without formal agreement.

Payment Terms
The payment terms clause specifies how and when the supplier will be compensated for their work. It outlines payment schedules, milestones, invoicing procedures, and any applicable penalties for late payments or non-compliance. Payment terms must be clear and agreed upon upfront to avoid misunderstandings. It can also define payment structures, such as fixed payments, milestone-based payments, or hourly rates.

Performance Standards and Deliverables
This clause defines the quality of work expected from the supplier and the deadlines for completing specific milestones. It sets performance metrics and outlines the criteria for success. In many cases, performance standards are tied to payment schedules, with the supplier receiving compensation upon meeting certain predefined deliverables.

Change Order Process
In most projects, changes to the scope of work will inevitably occur, whether due to unforeseen challenges, new requirements, or evolving client needs. The change order clause outlines the procedures for handling changes in the project. It specifies how changes will be documented, priced, and incorporated into the original contract. Without a clear change order process, both parties risk misunderstandings regarding changes to the project scope and costs.

Termination Clauses
A termination clause outlines the conditions under which either party can terminate the contract before the project's completion. It can include provisions for both voluntary and involuntary termination, specifying what constitutes a breach of contract or failure to perform. The clause should also cover what happens after termination, such as compensation for work completed, dispute resolution procedures, and the return of property or materials.

Dispute Resolution and Governing Law
This clause specifies how disputes will be resolved if they arise. It may include provisions for mediation, arbitration, or litigation. The governing law section identifies which jurisdiction's laws will apply in case of a legal dispute. This clause is essential for reducing the uncertainty around dispute resolution and avoiding prolonged legal battles.

Force Majeure
Force majeure clauses address unforeseen events such as natural disasters, war, or pandemics that may prevent a party from fulfilling their obligations under the contract. These clauses provide protection

to both parties by excusing them from liability under specific circumstances, such as events beyond their control that make performance impossible or impractical.

Indemnity and Liability

Indemnity clauses allocate responsibility between the buyer and supplier for damages, losses, or liabilities incurred during the project. They outline who will bear the cost of damages resulting from breaches of contract, negligence, or other legal violations. A well-drafted indemnity clause can limit the buyer's liability and protect them from claims that may arise during the project.

Confidentiality and Non-Disclosure

This clause is particularly important in projects that involve proprietary information, trade secrets, or sensitive data. The confidentiality and non-disclosure clause ensures that both parties agree to protect any confidential information exchanged during the project and prohibits them from disclosing it to third parties without consent. This clause safeguards intellectual property, trade secrets, and other sensitive business information from unauthorized disclosure.

Ensuring Fairness and Transparency in Agreements

In addition to addressing legal obligations, a well-drafted contract must foster fairness and transparency between the contracting parties. Ensuring that both the buyer and supplier are treated equitably in the agreement is essential for maintaining a positive working relationship and ensuring long-term success.

Clear and Unambiguous Language

Contracts should be written in clear, precise, and unambiguous language. Any vagueness or overly complex legal jargon can lead to confusion, disputes, and even legal challenges. Both parties must understand their rights and obligations without needing extensive legal interpretation.

Balance of Risk and Responsibility

A fair contract ensures that the allocation of risk is reasonable and balanced. In many cases, suppliers may seek to limit their liability for certain events, while buyers may want to protect themselves against delays or substandard work. A balanced approach ensures that neither party is unfairly burdened with too much risk. For example, if a supplier is responsible for delivering materials, they should not bear the entire risk of delays caused by a force majeure event.

Transparency in Costing and Payment Terms

Transparency in cost structures and payment terms is essential for preventing misunderstandings and disputes. Both parties should have a clear understanding of how costs are calculated, including any variables such as labor rates, material costs, or taxes. Additionally, payment terms should specify when payments are due and the conditions for invoicing, so there are no surprises on either side.

Use of Standardized Contract Templates

Standardized contract templates help ensure that essential clauses are not omitted and reduce the possibility of biased or overly favorable terms. Many industry associations provide standardized contracts that offer a balanced approach and are commonly accepted across projects of similar scope and complexity. Adopting these templates can enhance fairness and create a sense of mutual trust between parties.

Handling Intellectual Property and Confidentiality

Intellectual property (IP) and confidentiality are significant concerns in many projects, particularly in industries such as technology, research and development, and media. The handling of IP rights and confidentiality must be explicitly defined in the contract to prevent future disputes over ownership, usage, and protection.

Intellectual Property Clauses

In many projects, intellectual property is created or exchanged. IP clauses outline the ownership of any intellectual property that results from the project, including patents, trademarks, copyrights, and trade secrets. These clauses specify whether the intellectual property will belong to the buyer, the supplier, or be jointly owned.

For example, in software development projects, the client may want ownership of the source code, while the supplier may want to retain ownership of the tools or libraries used to build the product. The IP clause should clearly define the scope of use, any licensing arrangements, and whether the supplier has the right to use the intellectual property in future projects.

Confidentiality Agreements
Confidentiality clauses, often referred to as non-disclosure agreements (NDAs), protect sensitive information that is shared during the project. These clauses ensure that both parties agree not to disclose or misuse any confidential information obtained during the course of their collaboration. The definition of what constitutes confidential information should be comprehensive and precise, encompassing documents, data, communications, and trade secrets.

Confidentiality clauses should also define the duration for which the confidentiality obligation remains in effect. For example, even after the contract is completed, a supplier may be prohibited from disclosing confidential information for a specific period, such as three or five years. This extends protection well beyond the project's completion.

Safeguarding Trade Secrets
In many industries, protecting trade secrets is crucial to maintaining a competitive advantage. The contract should specify how trade secrets will be protected during the project, who has access to sensitive information, and the measures taken to prevent unauthorized disclosure or use.

Effective contract drafting and review are essential to the success of project procurement. By including key clauses that define the scope, payment terms, performance standards, and dispute resolution mechanisms, both the buyer and supplier can ensure that the project progresses smoothly. Equally important is ensuring fairness and transparency in the agreement, ensuring that both parties are treated equitably. Addressing intellectual property and confidentiality concerns in the contract also protects sensitive information and encourages innovation. By carefully crafting contracts that balance the interests of all parties, organizations can mitigate risks, foster long-term relationships, and ensure the successful execution of their projects.

13. Negotiation Skills for Project Procurement

Negotiation is a fundamental skill in project procurement, as it shapes the terms, conditions, and expectations between the buyer and the supplier. Effective negotiations can lead to favorable agreements that benefit both parties, ensuring the project progresses smoothly. This chapter explores the principles of effective negotiation, techniques for achieving win-win outcomes, and strategies for handling stalemates and conflicts.

Principles of Effective Negotiation

Effective negotiation is rooted in a few key principles that guide negotiators to achieve desirable results. These principles not only promote mutual respect between parties but also facilitate the development of agreements that are fair and beneficial for both sides.

Preparation and Planning

Preparation is the cornerstone of any successful negotiation. Before entering any negotiation, both the buyer and supplier need to understand their goals, constraints, and the potential value of the deal. This involves gathering relevant information, understanding market conditions, and identifying the key issues at hand. In project procurement, preparation includes assessing the project's scope, budget, timeline, and any specific requirements. Understanding the other party's needs and constraints is just as important. The more informed both sides are, the easier it will be to craft a mutually beneficial deal.

Setting Clear Objectives

Negotiators must have a clear understanding of their desired outcomes, both in terms of what they want to achieve and the limits they are willing to accept. In project procurement, this could involve setting clear expectations regarding price, timelines, scope of work, and deliverables. These objectives should be realistic, but negotiators must also have flexibility in mind in case the need for compromise arises. Well-defined objectives provide a roadmap that helps negotiators steer the conversation in a direction that supports their goals.

Building Relationships

While negotiations may sometimes be transactional, building strong relationships between the buyer and supplier can facilitate smoother negotiations. Relationship-building is particularly important in project procurement, where ongoing collaboration is often necessary. A positive relationship can foster trust, reduce misunderstandings, and help overcome potential conflicts. Trust encourages open communication and reduces the tendency for adversarial behavior, creating an environment where both sides feel heard and understood.

Understanding Interests, Not Just Positions

One of the most important negotiation principles is focusing on interests rather than positions. Positions are the demands or stances taken by each party, such as a specific price or a delivery deadline. However, interests are the underlying needs or desires that motivate those positions. For example, a buyer's position might be to secure a fixed-price contract, but their interest could be controlling costs and ensuring that the supplier delivers high-quality work on time. Similarly, a supplier's position might be to receive a higher payment for services rendered, but their interest could be securing long-term work. By focusing on interests rather than positions, negotiators can identify creative solutions that satisfy both parties.

Techniques for Win-Win Outcomes

Negotiation is not about "winning" at the expense of the other party. In project procurement, a win-win outcome means both the buyer and supplier leave the table satisfied with the agreement and feel they have achieved their objectives. Several techniques can help negotiators achieve such outcomes.

Mutual Gains Approach

The mutual gains approach is based on the idea that negotiators should search for options that allow both sides to benefit. This method involves openly discussing each party's interests, concerns, and priorities, leading to solutions that meet everyone's needs. For example, if the buyer is concerned about price and the supplier is concerned about securing fair compensation for their work, the parties might explore options such as extending the timeline or altering the scope of work to reduce costs. The mutual gains approach encourages collaboration, where both parties can identify creative ways to meet their objectives without forcing a compromise that leads to dissatisfaction.

Active Listening and Empathy

Effective negotiators practice active listening, which involves truly understanding the other party's concerns and interests. By focusing on the speaker and avoiding interrupting, negotiators can gather valuable insights into the needs of the other side. Empathy plays a key role in active listening, as it helps negotiators relate to the other party's perspective and respond thoughtfully. By acknowledging the other side's concerns and demonstrating a willingness to understand, negotiators create an atmosphere of respect and cooperation. This builds trust and makes it easier to reach mutually beneficial agreements.

Concessions and Trade-offs

Negotiation often requires making concessions to achieve a balanced outcome. The key to successful negotiation is making trade-offs where both parties give up something in exchange for something they value more. For example, the buyer might agree to a higher price in exchange for a quicker delivery timeline. Negotiators should approach concessions strategically—making small, non-critical concessions early on can help build goodwill, while more significant concessions should be made later in the negotiation process when both parties are committed to the deal. The goal is to create a fair exchange where each side perceives the overall agreement as balanced.

Problem Solving and Creative Solutions

Negotiators should look beyond the immediate issues and try to find solutions that provide value to both sides. This could involve brainstorming creative solutions or alternative proposals that satisfy both parties' underlying interests. In project procurement, issues such as delivery delays or budget constraints might seem like significant roadblocks, but a creative solution could involve adjusting the payment terms, extending timelines, or re-prioritizing project tasks. By focusing on solutions rather than problems, both sides can find ways to move forward that benefit the project and build a positive working relationship.

Handling Stalemates and Conflicts

Stalemates and conflicts are inevitable in many negotiations, especially in complex project procurement situations where both parties have competing interests. While it's important to strive for win-win outcomes, handling stalemates and conflicts effectively is essential to prevent a breakdown in negotiations.

Identifying the Source of the Conflict
Before trying to resolve a stalemate or conflict, negotiators must first understand its source. Conflict can arise due to misunderstandings, differing interests, unrealistic expectations, or poor communication. By identifying the underlying causes of the conflict, negotiators can address the root of the problem rather than simply treating the symptoms. Often, the conflict lies in unmet interests or poor communication, so it's crucial to have an open and honest conversation to get to the core issue.

Remaining Calm and Professional
In high-stress negotiations, emotions can run high, leading to frustration and escalating conflict. It's essential for negotiators to remain calm, composed, and professional throughout the process. Maintaining control over emotions helps prevent the negotiation from becoming adversarial and allows negotiators to focus on finding a solution. Taking a short break to cool down, if necessary, can provide a fresh perspective and reduce the intensity of the conflict.

Using a Third Party Mediator
If negotiations reach a stalemate and the parties are unable to resolve the issue on their own, bringing in a neutral third party can help. A mediator is an experienced professional who can facilitate communication between the parties, guide the conversation, and offer

suggestions for resolving the conflict. Mediators are trained to manage conflicts and help parties explore creative solutions. In project procurement, using a mediator can prevent delays and ensure the project remains on track.

Offering Solutions and Alternatives
In situations where both parties are stuck in a deadlock, it's important to be flexible and offer alternatives. For example, if the buyer and supplier disagree on price, the negotiator can propose alternative solutions such as deferred payments, partial deliveries, or performance-based payments. When both sides are stuck in a rigid position, presenting a variety of options allows them to choose the most viable solution. By being flexible and offering alternatives, negotiators demonstrate their willingness to work collaboratively and resolve the conflict.

Negotiation is an essential skill in project procurement, and mastering the principles, techniques, and strategies discussed in this chapter can lead to more successful, harmonious agreements. Effective negotiation involves thorough preparation, setting clear objectives, and focusing on mutual interests rather than rigid positions. Techniques for win-win outcomes, such as active listening, empathy, and creative problem-solving, help negotiators achieve balanced and mutually beneficial agreements. When faced with stalemates or conflicts, remaining calm, understanding the source of the issue, and seeking third-party mediation can help overcome barriers and reach a resolution. By developing strong negotiation skills, procurement professionals can ensure the successful completion of their projects while building long-term, positive relationships with suppliers.

14. Managing Contract Risks

In project procurement, managing contract risks is crucial for ensuring the success of a project. The ability to identify, assess, and mitigate risks through effective contract management can protect both parties from unexpected challenges. Effective risk management involves anticipating potential issues, clearly defining terms in the contract to allocate risks appropriately, and setting up mechanisms for resolving disputes before they escalate. This chapter explores the different types of contract risks, risk allocation strategies, and the importance of dispute resolution mechanisms to mitigate the impact of potential conflicts during the contract lifecycle.

Identifying and Mitigating Legal Risks

Legal risks in contract management are inherent due to the complexity of project procurement. These risks arise from the possibility that one party may fail to fulfill their contractual obligations, breach of contract, or the existence of unclear or ambiguous terms that lead to legal disputes. Identifying and mitigating legal risks is essential for minimizing potential liabilities and ensuring that the contract terms are enforceable.

Contractual Breach and Non-Compliance

One of the most common legal risks in project procurement is the risk of breach of contract. A breach occurs when one party fails to meet their obligations as outlined in the contract. This could include delays in delivery, substandard quality of work, failure to pay for goods and services provided, or the failure to meet other specified terms.

To mitigate the risk of contractual breaches, contracts must clearly outline the expectations, obligations, and performance criteria for both parties. Clear language that specifies deliverables, deadlines, and quality standards can minimize ambiguity. It is also important to include clauses that define the consequences of non-performance, such as liquidated damages, penalties, or termination clauses.

Lack of Compliance with Regulations and Standards

Legal compliance is another critical aspect of contract risk management. Projects often require adherence to industry-specific regulations, local laws, and international standards. Failing to comply with these regulations can lead to legal issues, fines, and the potential invalidation of the contract.

Mitigating compliance risks involves conducting thorough research into the legal requirements that apply to the project. Contract clauses should specify compliance with applicable laws and regulations, such as safety standards, environmental laws, and labor regulations. Ensuring that the contract parties understand and agree to these terms helps to prevent future legal complications.

Intellectual Property and Confidentiality Risks

Intellectual property (IP) and confidentiality risks are particularly relevant in projects involving technology, proprietary processes, or confidential information. Protecting IP and ensuring that sensitive information is not disclosed or misused is crucial for both the buyer and supplier.

Contracts should include clear terms about the ownership of intellectual property, licensing agreements, and restrictions on the use or distribution of confidential information. Non-disclosure agreements (NDAs) are commonly included to protect proprietary information from being shared with third parties. Clauses addressing intellectual property rights must define who retains ownership of new inventions or developments made during the project.

Risk Allocation Through Contract Terms

Risk allocation refers to how risks are distributed between the contracting parties in a way that is fair and manageable. The goal of risk allocation is to ensure that each party assumes responsibility for risks that are within their control, thus reducing exposure to unforeseeable events.

Risk Transfer and Indemnity Clauses

Risk transfer is one of the most effective ways to mitigate risks in a contract. Certain risks, such as insurance-related issues, can be transferred to third parties through indemnity clauses. These clauses specify that one party agrees to cover the other party for losses, damages, or legal claims that arise from certain events. For instance, a supplier may be required to indemnify the buyer in case of damages caused by defective goods or services.

By transferring specific risks, the contract parties can focus on managing risks that are within their ability to control. However, it is important to ensure that these clauses are legally enforceable and that the transferring party has the financial capability to honor the indemnity.

Limitation of Liability

Limiting liability is another key risk allocation strategy. Contracts often include clauses that cap the amount of compensation one party will owe the other in the event of a breach. For example, a supplier may limit its liability to the value of the contract or a specified amount. This protects both parties from being exposed to excessive financial loss due to an unforeseen event or error.

While limitation of liability clauses can provide certainty for both parties, they should be carefully drafted to ensure fairness. Excluding liability for certain types of damages, such as gross negligence or willful misconduct, may not be enforceable in some jurisdictions, so it is important to review these clauses carefully with legal counsel.

Force Majeure Clauses

A force majeure clause is a standard provision in many contracts that exempts parties from liability in the event of unforeseen circumstances that prevent them from fulfilling their contractual obligations. Force majeure events typically include natural disasters, pandemics, wars, strikes, or other major disruptions that are beyond the control of the contracting parties.

The inclusion of a force majeure clause helps to allocate the risk of extraordinary events that cannot be predicted or controlled. These clauses define the events that qualify as force majeure and set the procedures for notifying the other party and requesting an extension of time or other remedies. Properly drafted force majeure clauses help to protect both parties from liability while acknowledging the impact of uncontrollable events on the project timeline and deliverables.

Dispute Resolution and Conflict Management

Disputes are an inevitable part of the contract lifecycle, but effectively managing them through dispute resolution mechanisms can minimize disruptions and ensure the continued success of the project. The key to managing contract disputes is to establish clear procedures for resolving conflicts in the contract itself. These procedures should focus on negotiation, mediation, and arbitration before resorting to litigation.

Negotiation and Mediation
Negotiation is the first step in resolving any dispute. The goal of negotiation is to reach a mutually acceptable solution without escalating the issue further. In the event of a disagreement, both parties should engage in open and transparent discussions to understand the concerns of the other side and identify possible solutions.

If negotiation fails to resolve the dispute, mediation is the next step. Mediation involves bringing in a neutral third party to facilitate discussions between the conflicting parties. The mediator does not make decisions for the parties but helps them work through their differences and reach a compromise. Mediation is often less costly and time-consuming than litigation, making it an effective option for resolving disputes.

Arbitration
Arbitration is a more formal dispute resolution process in which a neutral third party, known as the arbitrator, hears both sides of the dispute and makes a binding decision. Arbitration is often quicker and more cost-effective than litigation, and it provides a private,

confidential resolution to conflicts. Many contracts include arbitration clauses that require parties to resolve disputes through arbitration rather than going to court.

While arbitration can offer a final and enforceable resolution, it is important to consider the potential costs and limitations of the process. Arbitrators may not have the same expertise as a court, and their decisions are typically final, with limited opportunities for appeal.

Litigation
Litigation is the final resort for dispute resolution when other methods such as negotiation, mediation, or arbitration fail. Litigation involves bringing the dispute before a court of law, where a judge or jury will make a decision. While litigation is often the most costly and time-consuming form of dispute resolution, it may be necessary when other methods have been exhausted.

Contracts should define the jurisdiction and venue for any litigation, specifying the legal system that will govern the dispute. This helps to clarify the procedural steps and ensures that both parties understand where and how legal action may be taken.

Effectively managing contract risks is crucial for ensuring the successful execution of a project. By identifying potential legal risks early in the contract lifecycle and allocating risks appropriately through clear contract terms, both parties can protect themselves from future disputes. Risk allocation strategies, such as indemnity clauses, limitation of liability, and force majeure clauses, help to ensure fairness and reduce exposure to unforeseen events. Furthermore, establishing dispute resolution mechanisms in advance, including negotiation, mediation, arbitration, and litigation, can facilitate the prompt resolution of conflicts, preventing delays and ensuring that the project remains on track. By prioritizing risk management in project procurement, both buyers and suppliers can safeguard their interests, foster positive working relationships, and contribute to the overall success of the project.

15. Closing Contracts and Final Deliverables

Closing a contract and ensuring that all deliverables are completed and meet the terms set out at the beginning of a project is an essential step in the procurement lifecycle. This phase can often determine whether a project is considered successful, both for the client and the vendor. The importance of this step lies in fulfilling the contractual obligations, reviewing performance, and documenting lessons learned for future improvements. Proper closure protects all parties involved, ensures compliance, and provides an opportunity for continuous improvement.

Ensuring Fulfillment of Contractual Obligations

Before closing a contract, it is vital to confirm that all terms and conditions stipulated in the contract have been met by both parties. This process requires a detailed review of the project against the original contract. In most contracts, the deliverables, timelines, and performance criteria are clearly outlined. The first step in the closing process is to ensure that the contractor has completed their responsibilities as agreed upon in the contract.

This process may involve:

> **Verification of Deliverables**: Reviewing the final deliverables to ensure they meet the agreed-upon quality standards and specifications. Each product or service provided should be examined in detail to confirm that the scope of work outlined in the contract has been fulfilled.

> **Compliance with Contract Terms**: The contract will typically outline deadlines, milestones, quality standards, and payment schedules. Ensuring that these milestones were met and that both parties adhered to these agreements is a critical part of closing the contract.

Final Inspections: This step often includes site visits or inspections where the project is evaluated against the deliverables agreed upon. Inspections help ensure that no elements are missing or deficient before the final acceptance.

Sign-Off from Stakeholders: Having both parties, including the project team, the vendor, and sometimes external auditors, sign off on the completion of work is a crucial part of confirming that all aspects of the contract have been met. This step might also require the project owner's or sponsor's formal acceptance of the deliverables.

Ensuring fulfillment also includes addressing any deficiencies or failures. If deliverables or milestones have not been met as per the contract, the next step is often to renegotiate timelines, costs, or quality standards before closing the contract. Depending on the situation, you might need to extend the contract, adjust payment schedules, or request remedial actions from the vendor.

Conducting Final Performance Reviews

After confirming the fulfillment of contractual obligations, the next step in contract closure is conducting a final performance review. Performance reviews assess how well the project or contract performed in terms of quality, timeliness, and budget, comparing it to what was initially agreed upon. This step helps both parties gauge whether the vendor delivered on their promises and allows them to identify areas of improvement for future collaborations.

Some key aspects to focus on during the performance review include:

Quality and Standards: Was the work completed to the required quality standards? Did the vendor meet the specifications set out in the contract? Performance metrics and

KPIs (Key Performance Indicators) can help measure the effectiveness of the vendor's work.

Timeliness: Was the project completed on time, or were there delays? If delays occurred, what were the reasons, and were they adequately communicated and justified?

Budget Adherence: Did the project stay within budget? Were there cost overruns, and if so, what caused them? This evaluation ensures that financial resources were appropriately allocated and managed throughout the procurement process.

Compliance with Legal and Ethical Standards: Did the vendor adhere to all legal, regulatory, and ethical standards outlined in the contract? Were there any breaches, and how were they handled?

A performance review is an opportunity to assess the vendor's strengths and areas for improvement. If the vendor has performed well, this review can serve as the foundation for a long-term relationship, whereas areas for improvement might require adjustments or corrective measures.

Performance reviews should involve feedback from various stakeholders, including project managers, team members, and external consultants. It's essential to gather both qualitative and quantitative feedback to gain a complete understanding of how well the contract and vendor performed.

Lessons Learned and Documentation

One of the most valuable outcomes of closing a contract is capturing and documenting lessons learned. The completion of a project provides a crucial opportunity to reflect on what went well, what didn't, and how the process can be improved in the future. The lessons learned phase helps ensure continuous improvement and can be a vital source of information for future procurement processes.

Some key lessons learned include:

What Went Well: Understanding what elements of the project or procurement process were successful helps ensure that best practices are continued in future contracts. For example, if a particular vendor delivered on time, within budget, and with excellent quality, it's worth noting this for future procurement decisions.

Areas for Improvement: Documenting areas where the procurement process or contract execution could have been handled better helps identify potential weaknesses. For instance, if delays in the delivery of services caused problems, understanding the root causes of those delays can prevent similar issues in the future.

Procurement Process Evaluation: Evaluating the procurement process itself is just as important. Were the procurement strategies effective? Did the tendering process work smoothly? Were the contract terms clear and enforceable? This analysis can guide improvements in the procurement function.

Risk and Issue Management: If risks or issues arose during the course of the project, documenting how they were handled (or not handled) provides valuable insights. Understanding how risks were identified, mitigated, and addressed can guide better risk management practices in the future.

Documenting lessons learned and having a clear process in place for this reflection can ensure that each project is a learning experience that can improve future projects. This documentation also serves as a resource for other teams or departments who might be working on similar contracts in the future.

Once lessons are documented, these insights should be shared with the relevant parties, including project managers, procurement teams, vendors, and other stakeholders. This feedback loop ensures that all parties can learn from the experience and improve their future collaboration.

Final Documentation and Records

The last step in closing contracts and finalizing deliverables is ensuring that all documentation related to the project and the contract is complete and properly archived. This documentation typically includes:

> **Signed Contracts and Amendments**: Copies of the signed contract, including any amendments made during the project, should be included in the project's final records.
>
> **Final Payment Records**: Any payment records, including invoices, receipts, and evidence of final payments, should be stored.
>
> **Performance Reports**: Final performance evaluations, vendor reports, and other relevant documents should be filed.
>
> **Compliance Documentation**: Any documents demonstrating that legal and regulatory requirements were met should be part of the final package.

Proper documentation serves several purposes, including:

> **Reference for Future Projects**: The archived contract, performance evaluations, and lessons learned are critical resources for future projects or vendor relationships. This provides valuable insights into how similar contracts should be managed moving forward.
>
> **Audit and Legal Protection**: Maintaining thorough records ensures that the project is transparent and can be audited. It also protects both the client and the vendor in case of any legal disputes after the contract is closed.

Stakeholder Communication: Final records should be communicated to all stakeholders involved in the project, ensuring they have a complete understanding of the project's outcomes.

Closing contracts and finalizing deliverables are crucial steps in the project procurement process. They involve ensuring that contractual obligations have been met, conducting performance reviews, documenting lessons learned, and ensuring all records are properly archived. This process not only protects both parties involved but also provides valuable insights for future projects. By reflecting on the project's successes and challenges, organizations can continuously improve their procurement processes and ensure that their future projects run smoothly, efficiently, and successfully.

Section 4: Execution and Control Chapter 16: Procurement Execution and Order Management   Issuing Purchase Orders and Managing

Section 4: Execution and Control

16. Procurement Execution and Order Management

The execution phase of procurement is crucial to ensuring that the materials, services, and products required for a project are delivered on time, meet the agreed-upon quality standards, and are properly managed from a logistics and inventory perspective. This phase includes issuing purchase orders, managing approvals, monitoring the delivery process, conducting quality control, and managing logistics and inventory. A well-managed execution phase ensures that the procurement process aligns with the project's objectives, avoids delays, and minimizes the risk of quality issues.

Issuing Purchase Orders and Managing Approvals

Once procurement requirements have been clearly defined and suppliers have been selected, the next step is issuing purchase orders (POs). The PO is the formal document used to request goods or services from a supplier, outlining the agreed-upon terms, conditions, quantities, and delivery schedules. A well-drafted PO serves as a legally binding agreement between the buyer and the supplier, providing clarity and protecting both parties in case of disputes.

The process of issuing purchase orders typically involves the following steps:

> **Creating Purchase Orders**: Based on the procurement plan, specific orders are created for the goods or services required. Each order should include detailed information, such as the description of the goods or services, quantity, agreed-upon prices, and delivery instructions. It's essential that these details align with the terms agreed upon during the vendor selection process.
>
> **Approval Workflow**: Depending on the organization's structure and internal policies, the PO may need to be approved by various stakeholders. This could include project managers, procurement officers, finance teams, or even legal

advisors, particularly for large or high-value orders. Having a clear and efficient approval workflow ensures that there are no delays in placing orders and that the terms are carefully reviewed before proceeding.

Communicating with Suppliers: After the PO is approved, it is sent to the supplier. It's crucial that suppliers acknowledge receipt of the order and confirm the delivery timelines, availability of goods, and any potential issues that could affect delivery.

Managing the approval process effectively is essential to avoid bottlenecks or errors. Having a streamlined process for issuing and approving purchase orders ensures the procurement cycle is efficient and transparent.

Ensuring Timely Delivery and Quality Control

Timely delivery and quality control are two critical factors that can determine the success of the procurement process. Delays in the delivery of goods or services can lead to project hold-ups, increased costs, and, in some cases, reputational damage. Similarly, failing to meet the agreed-upon quality standards can result in defects, rework, or even the need to switch suppliers mid-project.

Effective strategies for ensuring timely delivery and quality control include:

Monitoring Supplier Performance: Once the order is placed, it is important to monitor the supplier's performance in meeting delivery schedules. This may involve regular communication with the supplier, checking the order status, and conducting follow-ups to ensure that timelines are adhered to. Project managers should also verify that any potential delays are communicated promptly so that corrective actions can be taken.

Setting Up Milestones: Establishing clear delivery milestones or checkpoints can help ensure the supplier remains on track. These milestones allow project teams to assess whether products or services are being delivered as expected and identify any delays or issues early in the process.

Use of Vendor Management Systems (VMS): Many organizations utilize vendor management systems to track and manage the status of orders, deliveries, and performance. These systems help project managers maintain visibility over procurement operations and enable them to take proactive steps if issues arise.

Quality Control: Quality control is an essential aspect of procurement execution. Ensuring that the delivered goods and services meet the specified standards involves a rigorous process of inspection and testing. Depending on the complexity of the goods or services being procured, quality control measures may include:

> **Incoming Inspections**: Inspecting the goods upon delivery to ensure they match the specifications outlined in the PO. This could involve checking product dimensions, appearance, and functionality.
>
> **Third-Party Testing**: For specialized or high-value items, third-party testing may be used to verify that the product meets required standards. This could include safety certifications or compliance with regulatory standards.
>
> **In-House Testing**: In some cases, in-house teams may need to test the goods for functionality or compatibility with existing systems. This is especially important when procuring complex equipment or technology.

> **Defect Reporting and Rework**: If defects are found, it is essential to have a clear process for handling returns, replacements, or repairs. Communication with the supplier is key, and the supplier's response should be tracked to ensure that they meet their obligations under the warranty or service terms.

Ensuring that goods are delivered on time and meet the agreed quality standards is crucial for the success of the overall project. Delays or substandard products can lead to cost overruns, project disruption, and a loss of stakeholder confidence.

Managing Logistics and Inventory

Effective management of logistics and inventory is key to ensuring that procurement runs smoothly, especially in large projects that require multiple items to be delivered over an extended period. Without proper logistics management, delays, shortages, or excess stock can occur, which can affect the overall progress of the project.

Logistics Management

Logistics refers to the movement of goods from the supplier to the project site. Managing logistics involves ensuring that items are delivered to the right place, at the right time, and in the correct condition. The key elements of logistics management include:

> **Transportation Coordination**: Organizing the transportation of goods from suppliers to the project site or warehouse is a critical part of logistics management. Factors such as the size and weight of items, distance, and mode of transport (air, sea, road, or rail) must be considered when arranging transportation. Project managers should work closely with logistics providers to ensure timely and cost-effective deliveries.
>
> **Handling Customs and Regulatory Requirements**: For international procurement, logistics may involve navigating

customs regulations, tariffs, and import/export requirements. Understanding these rules and working with the supplier and logistics providers can help avoid delays or unexpected costs.

Tracking and Monitoring: Implementing a tracking system to monitor the movement of goods in real-time can provide transparency and allow project managers to anticipate and address any potential delays or issues with delivery. Many organizations use logistics management software to track shipments and manage documentation.

Inventory Management

Inventory management is essential to ensure that the right amount of stock is available at the right time. Proper inventory management can prevent both shortages and excess stock, both of which can lead to inefficiencies or unnecessary costs. Some important strategies for effective inventory management include:

Just-in-Time (JIT) Inventory: This strategy involves ordering materials only when they are needed, minimizing inventory holding costs. JIT can be particularly useful in projects with tight timelines or fluctuating demand.

Economic Order Quantity (EOQ): EOQ is a formula used to determine the optimal order quantity that minimizes total inventory costs, including ordering and holding costs. By calculating EOQ, project managers can ensure that they are ordering the right amount of materials, neither too much nor too little.

Safety Stock: Maintaining a safety stock of critical materials or components can help mitigate supply chain disruptions. Safety stock acts as a buffer to ensure that delays or disruptions in supply don't halt the project.

Stock Rotation and FIFO: In projects involving perishable goods or materials with limited shelf lives, implementing stock rotation systems like FIFO (First-In, First-Out) ensures that older stock is used first, preventing waste and shortages.

Inventory Audits: Regular inventory audits ensure that stock levels are accurate and that materials are readily available for use when needed. Audits also help identify discrepancies or losses, allowing the procurement team to take corrective action quickly.

In conclusion, procurement execution and order management are essential to the successful implementation of a project. By effectively issuing purchase orders, managing approvals, ensuring timely delivery, conducting quality control, and managing logistics and inventory, project managers can mitigate risks, avoid delays, and maintain the integrity of the project. Properly executed procurement processes contribute to the overall success of a project, delivering high-quality materials and services on time and within budget.

17. Monitoring and Controlling Procurement Activities

Monitoring and controlling procurement activities is a critical aspect of managing any project, ensuring that procurement processes are executed efficiently and effectively, within budget, and on schedule. By systematically tracking and controlling procurement activities, project managers can minimize risks, ensure compliance, and maintain alignment with project objectives. This chapter focuses on key tools and techniques for monitoring procurement activities, including the use of Key Performance Indicators (KPIs), procurement dashboards, reporting tools, and methods for identifying and resolving bottlenecks in the procurement process.

Using Key Performance Indicators (KPIs)

Key Performance Indicators (KPIs) are measurable values used to track the performance of procurement activities and ensure that they align with project goals. KPIs provide critical insight into the efficiency, cost-effectiveness, and timeliness of procurement operations. They allow project managers to identify areas for improvement and ensure that procurement activities are contributing to the success of the overall project.

Common procurement KPIs include:

> **On-Time Delivery**: This KPI measures whether suppliers deliver goods and services as per the agreed timelines. Monitoring on-time delivery helps ensure that procurement activities do not delay the overall project and that goods and services are available when needed.
>
> **Cost Variance**: Cost variance compares the actual procurement costs with the budgeted costs. This KPI helps project managers identify any cost overruns and take corrective action if procurement expenses exceed the planned budget.

Supplier Performance: This KPI evaluates the performance of suppliers based on factors such as quality, delivery times, and compliance with contract terms. Monitoring supplier performance helps ensure that suppliers meet expectations and that any issues are addressed promptly.

Procurement Cycle Time: This measures the amount of time it takes to complete a procurement cycle, from identifying needs to receiving goods or services. Shorter procurement cycle times contribute to overall project efficiency and help avoid delays.

Compliance Rate: Compliance with contractual agreements, legal standards, and organizational policies is essential for ensuring procurement activities meet required legal and regulatory frameworks. Monitoring compliance ensures that procurement practices follow established guidelines and mitigate risks.

Inventory Turnover Rate: This KPI tracks the rate at which inventory is used or sold over a period of time. High inventory turnover rates indicate efficient procurement processes and minimize holding costs.

KPIs should be defined at the beginning of the project and reviewed periodically to assess procurement performance. These indicators are invaluable for making data-driven decisions and improving procurement strategies.

Procurement Dashboards and Reporting Tools

Procurement dashboards and reporting tools are powerful resources for project managers to monitor procurement activities in real-time, track performance, and make informed decisions. Dashboards provide a visual representation of key procurement metrics and KPIs, while reporting tools offer detailed analysis and data insights.

Procurement Dashboards: A procurement dashboard consolidates real-time procurement data into a single view, providing project managers with a snapshot of procurement performance. Dashboards can display various KPIs, such as delivery performance, cost variance, order status, and supplier ratings. They help identify trends, highlight bottlenecks, and alert managers to potential issues. Dashboards can be customized to focus on specific procurement areas, such as supplier performance, order fulfillment, and budget management.

Modern procurement dashboards can integrate with procurement software and tools, providing live data and offering advanced analytics capabilities. For example, if on-time delivery drops below a certain threshold, the dashboard can alert project managers, prompting them to investigate the cause and take corrective actions.

Reporting Tools: While dashboards provide real-time insights, reporting tools offer in-depth analysis of procurement performance over a defined period. These tools allow project managers to generate reports based on specific KPIs or procurement activities. Reports can include detailed comparisons between planned and actual costs, supplier performance reviews, procurement cycle times, and compliance metrics.

Regular procurement reports can be scheduled to provide stakeholders with updates on procurement status. Detailed reports help in decision-making and allow project managers to demonstrate procurement effectiveness to stakeholders, ensuring transparency and accountability.

Automated Alerts: Many procurement dashboards and reporting tools include automated alert features. These alerts notify project managers of critical issues, such as overdue orders, escalating costs, or non-compliance with contract terms. Automated alerts help managers take proactive measures before minor issues escalate into major problems.

Integration with Other Project Management Tools: Procurement dashboards and reporting tools can be integrated with other project management tools, such as project scheduling software, financial management systems, and enterprise resource planning (ERP) platforms. This integration ensures that procurement data aligns with other project activities and enables comprehensive project monitoring.

The use of procurement dashboards and reporting tools enhances visibility, streamlines decision-making, and supports proactive management of procurement activities.

Identifying and Resolving Bottlenecks

Bottlenecks in procurement activities occur when certain processes or tasks hinder the smooth flow of the procurement cycle, leading to delays, increased costs, and reduced efficiency. Identifying and resolving bottlenecks is essential to maintaining project timelines and ensuring that procurement activities run smoothly.

Several common procurement bottlenecks include:

Supplier Delays: Suppliers may face challenges that prevent them from delivering goods or services on time, such as production delays, shipping issues, or unforeseen supply chain disruptions. These delays can have a cascading effect on the project schedule.

Approval Delays: Procurement processes often require multiple levels of approval, such as project managers, finance teams, and procurement officers. Delays in approval workflows can result in the late issuance of purchase orders and delay the entire procurement process.

Inventory Management Issues: Poor inventory management practices, such as overstocking or stockouts, can lead to procurement delays. Inefficient inventory tracking and poor demand forecasting can cause delays in obtaining required materials or lead to the need for expedited shipping, increasing costs.

Contract Negotiation Delays: Negotiating procurement contracts can be a time-consuming process, especially if there are disputes over terms, pricing, or delivery schedules. Contract negotiation delays can lead to significant hold-ups in procurement execution.

Inadequate Supplier Capacity: Sometimes, suppliers may not have the capacity to meet the demand, resulting in delays in production, delivery, or quality assurance.

To effectively identify and resolve bottlenecks, project managers should implement the following strategies:

Regular Monitoring: Ongoing monitoring of procurement activities through KPIs, dashboards, and reporting tools allows project managers to quickly identify delays or inefficiencies. By continuously reviewing procurement performance, project managers can spot bottlenecks early and take corrective actions.

Root Cause Analysis: When bottlenecks occur, it's essential to perform a root cause analysis to determine the underlying issue. For example, if a supplier is consistently late, the cause may be due to poor production planning, insufficient capacity, or transportation problems. Understanding the root cause helps determine the most appropriate solution.

Process Streamlining: Streamlining procurement processes, such as simplifying approval workflows or eliminating redundant steps, can reduce the time spent on administrative tasks and improve procurement efficiency.

Collaborating with Suppliers: Proactively working with suppliers can help mitigate delays. Regular communication, establishing clear expectations, and addressing any challenges that may arise can help ensure that the procurement process remains on track.

Contingency Planning: Having contingency plans in place can help address potential procurement bottlenecks. For example, maintaining backup suppliers or alternative sourcing options can ensure that the procurement process continues smoothly even if the primary supplier encounters difficulties.

Implementing Lean Principles: Lean procurement principles can be applied to eliminate waste and improve the efficiency of the procurement process. By analyzing each step in the procurement cycle and identifying areas of waste, project managers can streamline processes and reduce the likelihood of bottlenecks occurring.

In conclusion, monitoring and controlling procurement activities are integral to the success of any project. By using KPIs, procurement dashboards, and reporting tools, project managers can track performance, identify potential issues, and ensure that procurement processes align with project objectives. Identifying and resolving bottlenecks promptly minimizes delays, reduces costs, and contributes to the overall success of the project. Effective procurement monitoring and control enable project managers to maintain tight control over procurement activities and ensure that project goals are achieved on time and within budget.

18.Procurement Cost Management

Procurement cost management is a critical aspect of any project, as it directly impacts the project's budget, timelines, and overall success. Effective cost management ensures that procurement activities remain within the allocated budget, providing value while maintaining the quality and timelines of goods and services. This chapter delves into the key components of procurement cost management, including how to manage costs across the procurement lifecycle, the concept of Total Cost of Ownership (TCO), and strategies for cost reduction.

Managing Costs Across the Procurement Lifecycle

The procurement lifecycle spans from the identification of needs to the final delivery and closure of the contract. Throughout this lifecycle, various cost elements must be managed to avoid budget overruns, ensure value for money, and align procurement activities with the project's financial objectives. Proper management of procurement costs across the lifecycle requires careful planning, monitoring, and control.

> **Planning and Budgeting**: In the initial stages of procurement, it is essential to create a detailed procurement budget based on the estimated costs of materials, labor, services, and other project-related expenses. The procurement budget should be aligned with the overall project budget, and it should account for potential cost fluctuations due to market conditions, delivery timelines, and supplier negotiations. Accurate budgeting at this stage is crucial to setting realistic expectations and ensuring that procurement costs remain manageable.
>
> **Cost Estimation and Tracking**: During the procurement process, accurate cost estimation is necessary to ensure that suppliers provide competitive pricing, and that costs are accurately tracked over time. Costs should be regularly reviewed throughout the procurement process, from initial quotations through final invoices. Monitoring cost estimates and comparing them to actual expenditures helps identify cost

variances early and ensures that procurement activities remain within the set budget.

Cost Control and Reporting: As procurement activities progress, it is essential to control costs through monitoring, reporting, and regular assessments. Procurement professionals must track costs against the procurement plan and report any discrepancies to project managers and stakeholders. Effective reporting helps identify potential issues before they escalate, allowing for timely corrective actions. Additionally, procurement teams must continuously assess the value of the goods and services being procured relative to their cost, ensuring that they are receiving the desired return on investment (ROI).

Managing Change Orders: In many cases, procurement costs may be affected by changes in project scope, such as additional materials, changes in delivery timelines, or modifications in specifications. Change orders often lead to increased costs, so it is essential to manage these changes efficiently. Ensuring that all change orders are documented, justified, and approved can help control costs and minimize any negative impact on the overall budget.

Final Payment and Close-Out: As the procurement cycle concludes, the final costs are reconciled, and payments are processed according to the terms of the contract. This stage includes verifying that all goods and services have been delivered as agreed, checking that all cost-related documentation is in order, and ensuring that the final costs align with the agreed-upon terms. The procurement team must work closely with the finance and legal departments to ensure that payments are made accurately and on time, and that all contractual obligations are fulfilled before the procurement process is closed.

Throughout the procurement lifecycle, it is essential to establish strong cost management practices that include continuous tracking, reporting, and reviewing. This ensures that procurement activities stay within budget and that any potential risks to cost management are addressed promptly.

Analyzing Total Cost of Ownership (TCO)

The Total Cost of Ownership (TCO) is a comprehensive method of analyzing the full cost of procurement over the entire lifecycle of a product or service. TCO goes beyond the initial purchase price, taking into account all associated costs that can impact the overall budget, including acquisition, operational, maintenance, and disposal costs. By analyzing TCO, procurement managers can make more informed decisions and select suppliers that offer the best value over the long term.

TCO includes the following key elements:

> **Initial Purchase Price**: The upfront cost of acquiring goods or services is typically the first cost considered in the procurement decision. This is the most straightforward cost but does not reflect the total financial impact of the procurement.
>
> **Transportation and Logistics Costs**: These costs include the shipping, delivery, and handling fees associated with procuring goods or services. These costs can vary depending on the delivery method, distance, and any special handling requirements. Procurement managers must account for these costs to ensure accurate cost estimation and avoid surprises.
>
> **Operational Costs**: Operational costs are ongoing expenses related to the use of the goods or services being procured. For example, if procuring machinery or equipment, operational costs would include energy consumption, labor for operation, and any costs associated with downtime or inefficiencies.

Maintenance and Repair Costs: Over time, many goods and services require maintenance, repairs, or replacements. These costs should be considered when evaluating potential suppliers and product options. For example, a lower-cost product might require more frequent repairs or higher maintenance, increasing the TCO over time.

Training and Support Costs: When procuring complex systems or products, the cost of training staff and providing ongoing technical support must be included in the TCO analysis. While the initial purchase price may seem affordable, the long-term costs of training and support can significantly impact the total cost of ownership.

Disposal and End-of-Life Costs: Once the goods or services reach the end of their useful life, there may be disposal or recycling costs. These expenses should be factored into the TCO to avoid unexpected costs at the end of the procurement lifecycle.

Financing Costs: In some cases, financing costs such as interest or loan fees may be applicable, especially for large capital expenditures. These financing costs should be included in the TCO analysis to reflect the full financial burden of procurement.

By considering the full range of costs associated with procurement, the TCO approach allows project managers to make more strategic decisions. While an item may appear cheaper upfront, it might incur higher operational, maintenance, or disposal costs over time, making it a less attractive option compared to an alternative with a higher initial purchase price but lower long-term costs.

Strategies for Cost Reduction

Reducing procurement costs is a continual focus for procurement managers, as cost-saving measures can significantly impact the overall project budget. Various strategies can be employed to reduce procurement costs while maintaining quality, ensuring compliance, and meeting project objectives.

Strategic Sourcing: Strategic sourcing involves identifying the most cost-effective suppliers by evaluating factors such as price, quality, reliability, and delivery timelines. By adopting a strategic sourcing approach, organizations can negotiate better deals with suppliers, consolidate purchases, and secure favorable contract terms. For instance, bulk purchasing or long-term contracts can help reduce unit prices and improve supply chain efficiency.

Supplier Negotiations: Effective supplier negotiations can lead to significant cost reductions. Procurement managers should build strong relationships with suppliers and approach negotiations as a win-win scenario. Negotiation strategies such as volume discounts, early payment terms, and performance-based incentives can help drive down costs. Additionally, procurement professionals should aim to reduce unnecessary middlemen or intermediaries to improve cost-effectiveness.

Group Purchasing and Collaborative Buying: When multiple departments or projects require similar goods or services, group purchasing allows for collective buying power, leading to cost savings. Collaborative buying agreements with other organizations or industry peers can leverage economies of scale to secure better prices.

Process Efficiency: Streamlining procurement processes can reduce operational costs and eliminate inefficiencies. This includes automating procurement tasks such as purchase order creation, invoice processing, and supplier communications. Implementing an e-procurement system can help manage the procurement process more efficiently and reduce administrative overhead.

Outsourcing and Offshoring: For certain products or services, outsourcing to third-party vendors or offshoring to countries with lower labor costs can result in significant savings. However, it is important to balance cost savings with the quality of the goods or services and ensure that outsourcing does not negatively impact the project's success.

Cost Transparency: Creating a transparent procurement process where costs are clearly outlined and tracked can help identify opportunities for savings. Procurement professionals should encourage suppliers to provide a breakdown of their pricing structures and explore areas where cost reductions can be made without sacrificing quality.

Supplier Performance Management: Continuously managing supplier performance and fostering long-term relationships can drive cost reductions over time. By working closely with suppliers to improve efficiencies, reduce waste, and optimize delivery schedules, procurement teams can help minimize costs and enhance value.

Lean Procurement: Lean procurement focuses on eliminating waste, reducing inventory costs, and improving efficiency throughout the procurement process. By using lean tools such as value stream mapping, 5S, and Kanban, procurement teams can reduce unnecessary steps, cut down on excess inventory, and avoid overproduction, all of which contribute to cost savings.

In conclusion, procurement cost management plays a pivotal role in ensuring that a project is delivered on time, within budget, and with optimal value. By managing costs across the procurement lifecycle, analyzing the total cost of ownership, and implementing cost reduction strategies, procurement professionals can drive significant savings while maintaining quality and ensuring that project objectives are met.

19. Change Management in Procurement

Change is an inevitable aspect of any project. In procurement, change management becomes essential to ensure that adjustments to scope, timelines, budgets, and resources are effectively managed without disrupting the entire procurement process. This chapter focuses on handling scope changes and procurement adjustments, managing communication between teams and vendors, and mitigating disruptions during project procurement. It is important to understand that managing change effectively can lead to better procurement outcomes, increased supplier relationships, and successful project completion.

Handling Scope Changes and Procurement Adjustments

Scope changes are common in project procurement due to evolving project requirements, stakeholder requests, or unforeseen circumstances. Managing scope changes involves assessing the potential impact of these changes on the procurement process and adjusting procurement activities accordingly. When a scope change is proposed, it's essential to evaluate whether the change is reasonable and justifiable, its impact on the procurement budget, timeline, quality, and resources, and how it can be effectively incorporated into the procurement strategy.

> **Assessing the Change**: When a scope change request arises, the first step is to assess its necessity and impact. This includes understanding the specific changes required, whether they align with project objectives, and evaluating the potential consequences of making the change. In procurement, these changes may involve adjusting specifications, reissuing purchase orders, revising delivery schedules, or selecting new suppliers.

> **Impact on Budget and Timeline**: Changes in the scope of work often lead to changes in the budget and timeline. The procurement manager must review the proposed changes and work with the project manager to calculate the impact of these changes on the overall project budget. A cost analysis should be

done to ensure that the scope adjustment does not result in significant budget overruns or delays in procurement timelines. If adjustments are necessary, procurement managers should negotiate with suppliers to determine whether price increases or additional costs will occur due to the changes.

Revised Procurement Planning: If scope changes are approved, the procurement plan needs to be updated to reflect the new requirements. This could involve identifying new suppliers, revising the specifications of purchased goods or services, updating delivery schedules, and ensuring that any changes in project resources are factored into the procurement process. This updated plan should be communicated to all stakeholders, and necessary adjustments to procurement documentation, such as contracts or purchase orders, should be made accordingly.

Formal Change Control Process: To manage scope changes in a structured way, projects should have a formal change control process. This process includes clearly defining how scope changes will be identified, assessed, and implemented. Formal change requests should be documented, and all changes should be approved by the relevant stakeholders. This helps prevent unauthorized changes and ensures that the impact of any scope changes is thoroughly analyzed before being approved.

Managing Vendor Adjustments: When scope changes are made, suppliers may need to adjust their deliverables, timelines, or prices. Clear communication is essential to ensure that vendors understand the new requirements and can adjust accordingly. Procurement managers should discuss the changes with suppliers and determine if new contracts or amendments to existing contracts are required. It is also essential to assess whether the vendor's capacity and resources are sufficient to meet the revised requirements.

Managing Communication Between Teams and Vendors

Effective communication is crucial to managing procurement changes successfully. As scope changes or procurement adjustments are made, maintaining clear communication between internal teams (project managers, finance, legal, and procurement teams) and external vendors ensures alignment, understanding, and swift execution. Good communication mitigates misunderstandings, minimizes errors, and keeps the project on track.

Internal Team Coordination: Communication within the procurement team and across other departments involved in the project, such as project management, legal, and finance, is essential for a smooth procurement process. When procurement adjustments are required, the procurement manager should communicate clearly with the team members to ensure everyone understands the scope changes, timelines, and financial impacts. Regular cross-functional meetings should be held to review progress, discuss potential challenges, and ensure that all parties are aligned.

Vendor Communication: Effective communication with vendors is equally important. Once scope changes are identified, procurement managers must ensure that the vendors are informed promptly and clearly about any updates to the project requirements. This includes revising specifications, delivery schedules, or terms of service and ensuring that vendors are prepared for the changes. Transparent communication with vendors helps maintain strong relationships and ensures that vendors are on the same page regarding expectations.

Clear and Consistent Messaging: It's important to establish a clear communication plan for all stakeholders involved in the procurement process. This plan should outline who communicates with whom, what information needs to be shared, and how frequently communication should occur. Standardized communication templates, such as change order forms, email templates, and meeting agendas, help streamline communication and ensure that messages are consistent across all teams and vendors.

Managing Expectations: Scope changes often result in shifting expectations, and managing these expectations is crucial for maintaining strong working relationships. Procurement professionals must ensure that all stakeholders, including internal teams and vendors, understand the implications of the changes, including the potential impact on timelines, costs, and quality. It is also important to keep stakeholders informed about progress, any further changes, or delays.

Conflict Resolution: Changes in procurement can lead to disagreements or conflicts between teams or with vendors. These conflicts might arise due to misunderstandings, unmet expectations, or differing priorities. Procurement professionals should be equipped with conflict resolution skills, such as active listening, mediation, and compromise, to manage such situations effectively. Early identification of conflicts and addressing them promptly can prevent disruptions and maintain project momentum.

Mitigating Disruptions in Project Procurement

Disruptions in procurement can arise from various sources, including scope changes, supplier issues, logistical problems, or external market factors. These disruptions can cause delays, cost overruns, and project bottlenecks, making it essential for procurement professionals to develop strategies to mitigate and address these disruptions proactively.

Developing a Contingency Plan: A contingency plan is a proactive strategy that outlines actions to be taken in case of unexpected disruptions. This plan should include alternative suppliers, backup sources for critical materials, and strategies for dealing with delays or changes in project requirements.

Having contingency plans in place ensures that procurement can proceed smoothly even in the face of unforeseen circumstances.

Supplier Risk Management: Suppliers can sometimes face disruptions that impact their ability to deliver goods or services as agreed, such as production delays, transportation issues, or financial instability. To mitigate the risk of supplier-related disruptions, procurement managers should conduct thorough supplier risk assessments during the selection process and develop strong, collaborative relationships with key vendors. Building long-term partnerships and having a diversified supplier base can also reduce the impact of disruptions from a single source.

Technology and Automation: Leveraging technology and automation tools can help mitigate disruptions in procurement. Procurement software can streamline the order management process, track inventory, and provide real-time updates on supplier performance and inventory levels. By automating routine tasks such as order tracking, payment approvals, and contract management, procurement professionals can ensure that the procurement process remains efficient and less prone to disruptions.

Supply Chain Visibility: Greater supply chain visibility allows procurement managers to monitor potential issues in real-time and act quickly to resolve them. Using tools such as supply chain management software or procurement dashboards helps track delivery timelines, stock levels, and potential bottlenecks. This visibility allows for more effective decision-making and enables procurement professionals to address problems before they escalate into larger disruptions.

Communication During Disruptions: During disruptions, maintaining transparent and timely communication is essential to managing the impact on procurement. If issues arise, it is important to inform both internal teams and vendors about the situation and work together to find solutions. Open communication channels help reduce uncertainty and ensure that all stakeholders are aligned on next steps.

Monitoring External Factors: External factors such as market fluctuations, political instability, or natural disasters can affect procurement activities. Procurement managers should stay informed about potential disruptions in the broader environment that could impact suppliers, delivery times, or material costs. Monitoring these external factors allows for proactive mitigation strategies, such as adjusting sourcing strategies, renegotiating contract terms, or finding alternative suppliers.

In conclusion, change management in procurement is critical to ensuring that procurement processes remain efficient and that project goals are achieved despite challenges. By effectively handling scope changes, managing communication between teams and vendors, and mitigating potential disruptions, procurement professionals can help ensure that projects stay on track, on budget, and on time. With proactive planning, clear communication, and strong risk management, procurement can adapt to changes and continue to contribute to the success of the project.

Section 5: Advanced Topics in Project Procurement

20. Risk Management in Procurement

Procurement is an essential and complex part of project management, often encompassing the sourcing of materials, goods, and services from external suppliers. As with any area of project management, procurement carries various risks that can impact the successful delivery of the project. These risks may arise from several sources, including supplier failure, price fluctuations, regulatory changes, or logistical challenges. Effective risk management in procurement is critical to minimizing disruptions and ensuring that the procurement process contributes positively to the overall success of the project.

This chapter explores the identification of procurement risks, the development of contingency plans, and leveraging insurance as a tool for mitigating procurement risks. It is designed to provide professionals with advanced insights into how to navigate these challenges and secure the procurement process.

Identifying Procurement Risks

Risk identification is the first step in effective procurement risk management. Recognizing the risks inherent in procurement activities allows project managers and procurement professionals to develop strategies that can mitigate the impact of these risks. Procurement risks can be broadly classified into several categories:

> **Supplier Risk**: Supplier-related risks are among the most common in procurement. These risks arise when suppliers fail to meet their contractual obligations, either due to poor performance, financial instability, natural disasters, or political factors affecting their operations. For example, delays in delivery, subpar quality, or inability to meet volume requirements can disrupt the procurement process. Identifying reliable suppliers, assessing their financial health, and evaluating their operational capabilities are essential to mitigating this risk.

Price Fluctuation: Price volatility is another significant risk in procurement, especially when purchasing materials or commodities subject to market fluctuations. In industries such as construction, manufacturing, and technology, fluctuations in material costs can lead to budget overruns, delays, and conflicts. Suppliers' prices may increase unexpectedly due to changes in demand, currency fluctuations, or geopolitical events. Procurement professionals must anticipate these risks and consider incorporating price adjustment clauses in contracts to address future cost changes.

Contractual Risks: Procurement contracts are the backbone of the procurement process, and poorly structured contracts can expose the project to significant risks. Inadequate contract terms, ambiguities, and gaps in agreements can result in disputes, misunderstandings, or breaches. Furthermore, changes in legal frameworks or regulations can also create unforeseen risks that affect procurement agreements. To mitigate these risks, procurement managers must ensure that contracts are comprehensive, clear, and legally sound.

Supply Chain Risk: The global nature of modern supply chains increases the complexity and vulnerability of procurement activities. Disruptions in the supply chain due to transportation delays, strikes, port blockages, or adverse weather conditions can significantly impact the delivery schedule and cost of procurement. Supply chain risks also include reliance on a single supplier, which can lead to vulnerabilities if that supplier fails.

Regulatory and Compliance Risks: Compliance with regulatory frameworks is a critical aspect of procurement. Laws governing procurement vary by region and industry, and failure to comply with these regulations can result in legal consequences, fines, or contract cancellations. Changes in trade policies, tariffs, and taxes can also introduce uncertainty and risks into the procurement process. Procurement professionals must stay updated on relevant regulations and ensure that all contracts and transactions comply with legal requirements.

Logistical Risks: Logistics play a significant role in procurement, particularly in global supply chains. Risks related to transportation, storage, and handling of goods can disrupt the timely delivery of procurement materials. For example, transportation delays, damage to goods during shipment, and customs issues can all cause procurement delays. Effective risk management in logistics includes choosing reliable logistics providers and maintaining good visibility into the supply chain.

Developing Contingency Plans

Once procurement risks are identified, developing contingency plans is essential for mitigating these risks and minimizing their impact on the project. A contingency plan outlines the actions to be taken if a specific risk materializes. Having a well-thought-out contingency plan in place ensures that procurement activities can continue smoothly, even in the event of an unexpected disruption. Key elements of an effective contingency plan for procurement include:

Risk Assessment and Prioritization: The first step in contingency planning is to assess the likelihood and impact of identified risks. Not all risks carry the same weight, so it is important to prioritize them based on their potential to disrupt procurement activities and project outcomes. For example, a critical supplier failure may have a more significant impact than minor fluctuations in material prices. By understanding the risk landscape, procurement professionals can allocate resources to the most pressing risks.

Alternate Suppliers and Sources: One of the most effective ways to mitigate procurement risks is by diversifying the supplier base. Relying on a single supplier or source for critical materials increases the vulnerability to supply chain disruptions. As part of contingency planning, procurement managers should identify alternative suppliers and sources for key goods and services. This ensures that if a primary supplier fails, there is a backup option ready to step in.

Contract Flexibility: Contracts should be designed to account for changes in the procurement environment. Including flexibility clauses in procurement agreements allows for adjustments if issues arise during the execution of the contract. These clauses can cover areas such as price adjustments, delivery delays, or changes in scope. Procurement professionals can negotiate with suppliers to include terms that allow for adjustments, providing a safety net in case things do not go as planned.

Buffer Time and Inventory: When developing a contingency plan, it is crucial to factor in buffer time for procurement activities. If there are uncertainties around delivery schedules or potential delays, building buffer time into the procurement plan helps to avoid cascading project delays. Additionally, maintaining an inventory buffer can be useful in managing short-term disruptions. Stockpiling critical materials ensures that the project can continue even if delivery timelines are impacted.

Communication Protocols: A key component of contingency planning is establishing clear communication protocols. In the event of a disruption, it is vital to have a communication plan in place to quickly inform all relevant stakeholders, including internal project teams, suppliers, and customers. Timely and transparent communication can help minimize confusion and ensure that everyone is on the same page regarding the steps being taken to resolve the issue.

Regular Review and Update of Contingency Plans: Contingency plans should not be static; they must be regularly reviewed and updated based on changes in the procurement environment. As new risks emerge or existing risks evolve, the contingency plan should be adjusted to reflect these developments. Regular risk assessments and reviews of the procurement strategy help keep the plan relevant and effective.

Leveraging Insurance for Procurement Risk

Insurance is a powerful tool that procurement managers can use to mitigate certain types of procurement risks. By transferring the financial consequences of some risks to an insurance provider, organizations can reduce their exposure to potential losses. Procurement professionals must carefully assess the types of insurance that best fit their needs and the risks involved in their specific projects.

> **Types of Insurance for Procurement Risks**: Several types of insurance policies are available to protect against procurement-related risks. Some of the most relevant forms of insurance include:
>
> > **Supply Chain Insurance**: This type of insurance helps mitigate risks related to supply chain disruptions. It covers events such as natural disasters, transportation delays, and factory shutdowns that can affect the ability of suppliers to meet delivery schedules.
> >
> > **Product Liability Insurance**: If procurement involves the acquisition of goods that could potentially cause harm to users or clients, product liability insurance provides protection against claims arising from product defects or safety issues.
> >
> > **Cargo Insurance**: When goods are transported across long distances, cargo insurance provides coverage for any damage or loss that may occur during transit. This type of insurance is essential in protecting the goods being procured, especially in international shipments.

Professional Liability Insurance: If the procurement involves services or consulting, professional liability insurance can protect the project from claims of negligence, errors, or omissions in service delivery.

Evaluating Insurance Needs: Not all procurement risks can be covered by insurance, and insurance can come with significant costs. Therefore, procurement managers must carefully evaluate which risks are worth insuring against. It is crucial to perform a cost-benefit analysis to determine whether insurance provides adequate protection against potential losses and if the premiums are justifiable in the context of the project's overall budget.

Understanding Coverage and Exclusions: When selecting insurance policies, it is essential to understand the coverage details and exclusions. Insurance providers often have specific terms and conditions that determine what is covered under the policy and what is excluded. Procurement professionals must ensure that their policies provide adequate protection for the identified risks and that any exclusions are understood upfront.

Claims Management: In the event of a procurement-related risk materializing, procurement professionals must understand how to file claims and manage the claims process with insurance providers. Having a clear process for reporting and managing claims ensures that the organization can recover losses in a timely manner and avoid delays in project execution.

Procurement risk management is a vital component of the procurement process that ensures the stability and success of projects. By identifying procurement risks early, developing comprehensive contingency plans, and leveraging insurance to mitigate potential financial losses, procurement professionals can protect their projects from unexpected disruptions. These strategies help create a more resilient procurement system, allowing organizations to respond effectively to challenges and maintain progress toward project completion. By adopting a proactive approach to risk management, procurement professionals can minimize the negative impacts of risks and enhance the overall performance of the procurement process.

21.Sustainable Procurement Practices

In recent years, sustainable procurement has become an essential focus for businesses across the globe. Organizations are increasingly realizing that their procurement decisions do not only impact their bottom line but also have significant social, environmental, and ethical implications. Sustainable procurement involves integrating environmental, social, and economic factors into procurement decisions in order to create long-term value. It ensures that the products and services sourced have minimal negative impact on the environment, support social equity, and uphold ethical practices.

This chapter explores sustainable procurement practices, including green procurement and environmental considerations, social and ethical responsibilities in procurement, and the principles of a circular economy. It provides procurement professionals with the tools and knowledge to implement sustainability into their procurement processes effectively.

Green Procurement and Environmental Considerations

Green procurement, often referred to as environmentally responsible procurement, focuses on sourcing products and services that have a minimal impact on the environment. The goal is to reduce the ecological footprint of the organization and contribute positively to the environment by considering sustainability in the procurement process.

> **Defining Green Procurement**: Green procurement refers to the acquisition of goods and services that have been produced, used, or disposed of in an environmentally friendly manner. This involves considering factors such as the materials used in production, energy efficiency, resource conservation, waste reduction, and the overall lifecycle impact of products.

Green procurement not only focuses on reducing environmental impact but also on sourcing sustainable alternatives that contribute to the reduction of carbon emissions, pollution, and waste. For example, choosing energy-efficient products or sourcing raw materials from sustainable sources can play a significant role in reducing an organization's environmental impact.

Key Environmental Criteria: There are several key environmental criteria that procurement professionals can use to assess products and suppliers for green procurement:

> **Energy Efficiency**: Products that use less energy over their lifecycle, such as energy-efficient machinery or LED lighting, can significantly reduce energy consumption and lower operating costs.

> **Sustainable Materials**: Sourcing materials from renewable or responsibly managed sources, such as FSC-certified wood, can reduce environmental degradation.

> **Waste Reduction**: Products that can be recycled, have minimal packaging, or are reusable help minimize waste generation and contribute to more sustainable disposal practices.

> **Carbon Footprint**: The carbon emissions produced during manufacturing, transportation, and product use should be evaluated. Organizations can choose suppliers that have effective carbon reduction strategies in place.

Benefits of Green Procurement: Adopting green procurement practices offers a wide range of benefits. These include reducing environmental impact, improving organizational reputation, ensuring regulatory compliance, and potentially lowering costs through energy savings, waste reduction, and operational efficiencies. Moreover, by focusing on green procurement, businesses can contribute to the global effort of mitigating climate change and achieving sustainable development goals.

Barriers to Green Procurement: Despite its benefits, implementing green procurement can face several challenges. These include higher initial costs of green products, limited availability of sustainable suppliers, lack of knowledge or awareness about green options, and difficulty in measuring the environmental impact of products. Overcoming these barriers requires education, collaboration, and long-term commitment from organizations to integrate sustainability into their procurement processes.

Social and Ethical Responsibilities in Procurement

Social and ethical considerations are a crucial part of sustainable procurement. Ethical procurement practices ensure that the organization's supply chain respects human rights, promotes fair labor practices, and supports social equity.

Labor Rights and Fair Trade: Procurement professionals must ensure that their suppliers adhere to fair labor standards. This includes providing safe working conditions, fair wages, and reasonable working hours. Additionally, procurement decisions should promote fair trade practices, where suppliers from developing countries are paid fairly for their goods and services. Ethical procurement seeks to avoid exploiting workers and to prevent human rights abuses such as child labor, forced labor, and unsafe working conditions.

Supplier Diversity and Inclusion: Ethical procurement promotes supplier diversity by encouraging organizations to source products and services from a wide range of suppliers, including small businesses, minority-owned businesses, and women-owned businesses. By supporting a diverse group of suppliers, organizations contribute to economic inclusion and social equity. Supplier diversity can also foster innovation and creativity within the supply chain, providing access to new products, services, and ideas.

Transparency and Traceability: Transparency in procurement is critical to ensuring ethical practices. Procurement professionals should require suppliers to provide information about the origin of materials, the production processes, and the working conditions within their facilities. Traceability helps organizations ensure that their supply chains are free from unethical practices, such as human rights violations or environmental harm.

Corporate Social Responsibility (CSR): Many companies incorporate CSR into their procurement practices by selecting suppliers who align with their values and social objectives. For example, an organization may prioritize working with suppliers who engage in charitable activities, support local communities, or have environmentally conscious operations. Procurement professionals should evaluate potential suppliers not only for the quality and price of their products but also for their broader social and ethical contributions.

Anti-Corruption and Bribery: Procurement professionals must also ensure that their suppliers adhere to anti-corruption and anti-bribery regulations. This includes ensuring that suppliers do not engage in illegal or unethical practices, such as bribing government officials or other stakeholders to secure contracts. Ethical procurement involves working with suppliers who are committed to integrity and transparency in their business operations.

Circular Economy and Supplier Accountability

The concept of the circular economy focuses on reducing waste and maximizing the use of resources. In the context of procurement, a circular economy emphasizes the reuse, refurbishment, recycling, and sustainable disposal of materials and products.

Principles of a Circular Economy: The circular economy is based on three fundamental principles:

Design for Longevity: Products should be designed to last longer and be repairable, rather than being disposed of after a short period of use. This includes designing products that can be easily disassembled for reuse or recycling.

Reuse and Recycle: Rather than discarding products at the end of their lifecycle, they should be reused or repurposed. For example, electronic goods can be refurbished and resold, and industrial equipment can be refurbished and put back into use.

Resource Efficiency: Procurement practices should focus on reducing resource consumption and ensuring that products and materials are used efficiently throughout their lifecycle. This can involve sourcing materials that are easily recyclable or choosing products with minimal environmental impact.

Supplier Accountability: In a circular economy, suppliers play a key role in ensuring that products are designed, produced, and disposed of in a sustainable manner. Procurement professionals must hold suppliers accountable for the sustainability of their practices. This can include assessing suppliers' waste management processes, resource usage, and their contribution to reducing carbon emissions.

Accountability extends to ensuring that suppliers provide products that can be reused or recycled. For example, a procurement manager might choose a supplier that offers products made from recycled materials or is committed to taking back used products for recycling at the end of their useful life.

Collaboration with Suppliers: Achieving a circular economy requires close collaboration between buyers and suppliers. Procurement professionals should engage suppliers in discussions about sustainability goals and work together to find innovative solutions to reduce waste, reuse materials, and recycle products. This could involve designing new products with fewer materials, reducing packaging waste, or implementing a closed-loop supply chain where products are returned and reused.

Barriers to Circular Economy Adoption: Despite its potential, the circular economy faces several challenges in procurement. These include the higher upfront costs of sustainable products, lack of infrastructure for recycling or repurposing materials, limited availability of suppliers offering circular solutions, and a lack of awareness or understanding of circular economy principles. Overcoming these barriers requires a shift in mindset from short-term cost considerations to long-term sustainability goals.

Sustainable procurement practices are essential for organizations aiming to reduce their environmental footprint, uphold social responsibility, and contribute positively to society. By adopting green procurement, ensuring ethical practices in supplier relationships, and embracing the principles of a circular economy, procurement professionals can significantly enhance the sustainability of their supply chains. Sustainable procurement not only supports environmental and social goals but also offers long-term business benefits, including cost savings, improved reputation, and greater resilience. As sustainability becomes increasingly important in the global marketplace, integrating these practices into procurement strategies will be critical to the success and growth of organizations in the future.

22.Technology in Project Procurement

The landscape of project procurement is evolving rapidly, driven by advancements in technology. The traditional methods of procurement that relied heavily on manual processes are increasingly being replaced by digital solutions designed to improve efficiency, reduce errors, enhance transparency, and streamline workflows. In this chapter, we explore the role of automation and artificial intelligence (AI) in procurement, the potential of blockchain technology for ensuring procurement transparency, and the significance of procurement software and tools in modern procurement practices. These technological innovations are transforming the procurement function and shaping the future of project procurement management.

Role of Automation and AI in Procurement Processes

Automation and AI are two of the most significant technological innovations that are reshaping project procurement. These technologies enable procurement professionals to optimize their workflows, make data-driven decisions, and reduce administrative overhead, allowing them to focus on more strategic tasks. Automation and AI enhance procurement processes by improving speed, accuracy, and consistency, while also driving down operational costs.

> **Automation in Procurement**: Automation in procurement refers to the use of technology to perform repetitive, manual tasks without human intervention. These tasks can include activities such as order placement, invoice processing, supplier management, and reporting. Automation tools help streamline procurement workflows, reduce human error, and improve the overall efficiency of the procurement cycle.
>
> For example, automated purchase order systems can generate and send orders to suppliers automatically when stock levels fall below a certain threshold. This reduces the time spent manually tracking inventory and placing orders, ensuring that procurement decisions are made promptly.

Automation also plays a critical role in contract management. By automating contract creation, tracking, and renewal processes, organizations can avoid the risk of missing key contract deadlines and ensure that they are compliant with the terms agreed upon with suppliers. Additionally, automated systems help ensure that procurement teams adhere to budgets and timelines by providing real-time insights into purchasing activities.

Artificial Intelligence in Procurement: AI goes beyond automation by adding the ability to analyze large datasets, identify patterns, and make predictions based on historical data. In procurement, AI can be used to enhance decision-making, improve forecasting, and optimize supplier selection. AI-powered procurement systems can analyze past purchasing data to predict future demand, helping organizations better manage inventory levels and reduce the risk of stockouts or overstocking.

AI can also assist with supplier selection and performance evaluation. By analyzing historical supplier data, AI tools can assess supplier reliability, quality, and delivery performance. AI can also help identify risks in the supply chain by recognizing patterns that could indicate potential disruptions, such as delays in production or transportation.

Moreover, AI-powered chatbots can improve communication with suppliers and internal teams. These chatbots can answer queries, provide updates on procurement status, and even assist in negotiating terms, further reducing the workload of procurement teams.

Enhanced Decision-Making: AI enhances decision-making in procurement by enabling data-driven insights. By analyzing historical data, AI algorithms can identify trends and predict future procurement needs, helping procurement managers make informed decisions. For instance, AI can predict when certain products or services will be in high demand, allowing procurement teams to adjust their strategies and secure better prices or avoid delays.

Additionally, AI can support procurement teams in supplier negotiations. By analyzing pricing models, historical cost trends, and supplier performance, AI tools can help procurement professionals identify the best suppliers, understand pricing patterns, and negotiate more favorable terms.

Blockchain for Procurement Transparency

Blockchain technology, which underpins cryptocurrencies like Bitcoin, has potential applications beyond financial transactions. In procurement, blockchain is used to ensure transparency, security, and traceability in the supply chain. Blockchain's decentralized and immutable nature makes it an ideal solution for addressing some of the key challenges faced by procurement teams, including fraud prevention, supplier verification, and contract enforcement.

Enhancing Transparency and Trust: One of the primary benefits of blockchain in procurement is its ability to increase transparency. By recording every transaction on a public ledger, blockchain allows all stakeholders to have access to the same information, ensuring that all procurement activities are fully traceable. This transparency can be especially useful when managing complex, multi-party contracts or cross-border transactions.

Blockchain's ability to provide a permanent, immutable record of all transactions helps prevent fraud and reduce the risk of discrepancies in procurement activities. Suppliers, buyers, and procurement teams can all access real-time data about a product's journey from source to end customer, ensuring that all parties are adhering to contractual terms.

Smart Contracts: Another key feature of blockchain technology is the ability to create smart contracts. These are self-executing contracts with the terms of the agreement directly written into code. Smart contracts automatically execute actions when predefined conditions are met, such as releasing payments to a supplier once goods are delivered, or updating inventory levels when a purchase is made.

Smart contracts reduce the need for intermediaries, minimize human error, and ensure that all parties comply with the agreed-upon terms. For example, in a procurement scenario, a smart contract could trigger automatic payment to a supplier upon delivery, and the transaction would be recorded on the blockchain, making it transparent and verifiable.

Supply Chain Traceability: Blockchain allows for greater supply chain traceability, which is crucial for industries such as pharmaceuticals, food, and electronics, where product authenticity and compliance with regulations are paramount. Blockchain enables the tracking of goods from their origin to the final consumer, providing proof of origin, authenticity, and compliance with safety standards. This transparency helps organizations identify potential risks, such as counterfeit products or substandard materials, and take action to mitigate them.

Additionally, blockchain enhances the ability to track and trace the environmental impact of products throughout their lifecycle. Companies can verify whether a supplier is adhering to sustainable practices, ensuring that they meet the organization's environmental and social responsibility standards.

Procurement Software and Tools

As the procurement function becomes more complex and data-driven, procurement software and tools have become indispensable for managing the entire procurement lifecycle. These tools provide procurement teams with real-time insights, streamline administrative processes, and improve collaboration with suppliers and internal stakeholders.

Procurement Management Systems (PMS): Procurement management software is designed to automate and streamline various procurement tasks, such as requisitioning, sourcing, supplier management, purchasing, and invoicing. These tools help procurement teams manage all aspects of the procurement process in one integrated system, providing greater visibility, control, and efficiency.

A robust PMS enables procurement teams to track orders, monitor supplier performance, and ensure that procurement activities align with the organization's objectives and budget. These systems often integrate with other enterprise software, such as Enterprise Resource Planning (ERP) systems and supply chain management tools, to provide end-to-end visibility across the organization's procurement operations.

E-Sourcing Tools: E-sourcing platforms are used to manage the sourcing process, including supplier discovery, request for proposal (RFP) issuance, and bid evaluation. These tools allow procurement teams to reach a wider pool of suppliers, streamline the bidding process, and compare supplier offers more effectively. E-sourcing platforms can also automate the negotiation process, using algorithms to find the most competitive pricing and terms.

Additionally, e-sourcing tools often include functionality for managing supplier relationships, tracking performance, and conducting supplier evaluations. These features help procurement teams make data-driven decisions when selecting suppliers, ensuring that the organization works with the most reliable and cost-effective partners.

Spend Analysis Software: Spend analysis tools allow procurement teams to gain visibility into the organization's spending patterns and identify opportunities for cost savings. These tools aggregate data from various procurement activities, categorize spending, and provide insights into spending trends and supplier performance.

Spend analysis software helps procurement teams identify areas of inefficiency, such as maverick spending or excessive costs with certain suppliers. By analyzing historical spending data, organizations can negotiate better contracts, optimize supplier relationships, and improve procurement strategies.

Supplier Relationship Management (SRM) Systems: Supplier relationship management (SRM) software helps organizations manage their relationships with suppliers, ensuring that procurement teams maintain strong, collaborative partnerships. SRM systems enable procurement professionals to monitor supplier performance, track delivery schedules, manage contract compliance, and assess risks.

By providing a centralized repository of supplier information, SRM systems help procurement teams maintain accurate records, streamline communication, and improve supplier collaboration. These tools also enable procurement teams to assess supplier risks and identify potential issues early in the process, helping to mitigate disruptions in the supply chain.

The integration of technology into project procurement is no longer a luxury but a necessity. Automation and AI are revolutionizing procurement processes by streamlining tasks, improving decision-making, and enabling data-driven insights. Blockchain technology is enhancing transparency, security, and traceability in the procurement process, while procurement software and tools are centralizing procurement activities and providing real-time visibility across the supply chain.

By adopting these technologies, organizations can improve procurement efficiency, reduce risks, and create more transparent, sustainable, and cost-effective procurement strategies. As technology continues to evolve, procurement professionals must stay informed about the latest advancements and adopt the tools that best align with their organization's goals and objectives.

23.Global Procurement in Projects

In today's interconnected world, global procurement has become an integral part of project management. Companies increasingly source materials, services, and labor from international suppliers to take advantage of competitive pricing, specialized expertise, or to meet project-specific needs. However, managing cross-border procurement comes with its unique challenges, including handling cultural differences, navigating complex trade regulations, and overcoming communication barriers. Understanding how to navigate these issues effectively is critical for procurement professionals involved in global projects.

This chapter explores the key aspects of global procurement in projects, focusing on managing cross-border suppliers, handling cultural differences and communication barriers, and navigating international trade and customs regulations.

Managing Cross-Border Suppliers

Managing cross-border suppliers is often one of the most complex aspects of global procurement. The nature of international supply chains means that procurement professionals must deal with various legal, financial, and logistical considerations. The key challenges in managing cross-border suppliers include:

> **Supplier Selection and Risk Management**: One of the first steps in global procurement is selecting the right suppliers. This can be more difficult than sourcing from local vendors due to different business practices, currencies, and legal systems. It is essential to conduct thorough due diligence on potential suppliers, which should include evaluating their financial stability, quality standards, reliability, and past performance in international supply chains.
>
> In addition, assessing and mitigating the risks associated with global procurement is crucial. Supply chain risks include geopolitical instability, currency fluctuations, customs delays, and changes in international trade regulations. Procurement

teams can mitigate these risks by diversifying suppliers, using forward contracts to hedge currency risks, and developing contingency plans for unexpected delays or disruptions.

Legal and Regulatory Compliance: Global procurement often requires compliance with international laws and regulations. This can include export control laws, product safety standards, labor laws, and environmental regulations that differ by country. Understanding these legal requirements is essential to avoid costly fines, delays, or compliance issues.

Contractual agreements should clearly define the terms of engagement with cross-border suppliers. These contracts should address areas such as dispute resolution mechanisms, warranties, penalties for non-performance, and terms related to compliance with international regulations.

Logistics and Delivery Management: Managing logistics for cross-border suppliers involves complex coordination between multiple parties, including suppliers, freight forwarders, and customs authorities. Shipping times, transportation costs, and potential delays due to customs procedures can affect project timelines and budgets. Procurement teams must work closely with logistics experts to ensure that goods are delivered on time, at the right cost, and in the required condition.

To streamline logistics and minimize delays, procurement professionals can use technologies such as transportation management systems (TMS) and track-and-trace software, which provide real-time visibility into shipments, helping to anticipate and resolve issues before they affect the project.

Handling Cultural Differences and Communication Barriers

Effective communication is essential when managing international suppliers. However, cultural differences and language barriers can present significant challenges in cross-border procurement.

Misunderstandings, misinterpretations, and differences in work ethics can lead to delays, errors, and strained relationships. Therefore, it is important to be proactive in addressing these issues.

Cultural Sensitivity and Awareness: Cultural differences can impact negotiations, decision-making processes, and daily operations. For example, in some cultures, decisions are made through consensus, while in others, they are made by a single individual. Additionally, attitudes toward time, deadlines, and formalities can vary significantly across countries.

Procurement professionals should take the time to learn about the cultural norms and practices of their international suppliers. This includes understanding how to build trust, appropriate forms of communication, and decision-making processes within the local business culture. Establishing a positive, respectful relationship with suppliers is essential for long-term collaboration.

Communication Styles: Language barriers can complicate negotiations, contracts, and day-to-day communication. Procurement teams must ensure that clear and consistent communication is maintained with suppliers, using simple language, avoiding jargon, and confirming understanding of key points.

In addition to language barriers, there may be differences in communication styles. In some cultures, direct communication is preferred, while in others, indirect communication is more common. Understanding these nuances can help prevent miscommunication and ensure that expectations are clearly defined on both sides.

Conflict Resolution: Disputes are an inevitable part of cross-border procurement, and cultural differences can sometimes exacerbate conflicts. To manage potential conflicts effectively, it is important to establish a structured approach to conflict resolution early on. This might include developing a clear dispute resolution clause in contracts, which specifies how disagreements will be addressed—whether through negotiation, mediation, arbitration, or litigation.

Procurement professionals should also be prepared to adapt their negotiation and conflict resolution strategies to accommodate different cultural norms, ensuring that the approach used is respectful and effective.

Navigating International Trade and Customs

International trade and customs regulations are another key area of focus in global procurement. These regulations vary significantly from one country to another, and navigating them effectively requires a deep understanding of the legal and procedural requirements for importing and exporting goods.

> **Customs Procedures**: Customs procedures are one of the most significant challenges in global procurement. Every country has its own rules and processes for importing goods, and failure to comply with these regulations can result in delays, fines, or even confiscation of goods. To minimize delays, procurement teams need to work closely with customs brokers or freight forwarders who are familiar with the specific requirements of the destination country.
>
> Key areas that must be managed include tariff classifications, import duties, and product certifications. Procurement professionals should also ensure that the necessary documentation—such as invoices, bills of lading, and certificates of origin—are accurate and complete to avoid customs delays.
>
> **Tariffs and Duties**: Tariffs and duties are taxes levied on imported goods, and they can significantly impact the cost of procurement. These duties vary depending on the country of

origin, the type of product, and the value of the goods being imported. It is essential for procurement professionals to understand the tariff codes for the products they are sourcing, as well as any preferential trade agreements that may reduce or eliminate duties.

In some cases, procurement teams can work with suppliers to explore the potential for duty drawback programs, which allow companies to reclaim some of the duties paid on goods that are later exported. Additionally, using bonded warehouses or free trade zones can help reduce the financial impact of import duties.

International Trade Agreements: Many countries are part of international trade agreements that establish specific trade rules and tariffs between member nations. For example, the North American Free Trade Agreement (NAFTA) between the United States, Canada, and Mexico, or the European Union's trade agreements with non-EU countries, can provide preferential terms for procurement activities within the region.

Procurement professionals need to stay informed about the international trade agreements that apply to their projects and ensure that they take full advantage of any preferential terms that may apply. These agreements can help reduce costs and simplify the procurement process, but it is important to remain aware of any changes to trade policies or tariffs that may affect the project.

Import and Export Regulations: Import and export regulations vary widely between countries and can change rapidly in response to political or economic shifts. Procurement professionals need to stay up-to-date with the latest regulations in the countries where they are sourcing goods. This includes ensuring compliance with sanctions, embargoes, and export control laws that may restrict the flow of goods to certain regions or countries.

Additionally, some countries require specific product certifications, such as CE marking for products sold in the European Union or UL certification for electrical products in the United States. Ensuring that products meet the required standards and certifications is crucial for avoiding compliance issues and ensuring the timely delivery of goods.

Global procurement in projects offers significant opportunities for cost savings, access to specialized expertise, and flexibility in sourcing materials and services. However, it also presents unique challenges that require careful management of cross-border suppliers, cultural differences, and international trade and customs regulations.

Procurement professionals must develop a strong understanding of the complexities involved in managing global supply chains, from selecting suppliers and negotiating contracts to ensuring compliance with legal and regulatory requirements. By leveraging effective communication strategies, addressing cultural differences, and staying informed about global trade policies, procurement teams can successfully navigate the complexities of international procurement and contribute to the successful delivery of global projects.

24. Procurement Lessons from Real-World Projects

Procurement plays a critical role in the success of any project, whether it is in construction, manufacturing, IT, or any other industry. While the principles of procurement remain largely constant, each project presents its own unique challenges and lessons. Learning from real-world case studies, both successes and failures, helps procurement professionals gain insights into how to navigate complex procurement situations and avoid pitfalls. This chapter will explore case studies of procurement successes and failures, analyze procurement challenges in complex projects, and apply best practices from diverse industries to improve procurement outcomes.

Case Studies of Procurement Successes and Failures

Success: The Sydney Opera House

One of the most well-known procurement success stories is the construction of the Sydney Opera House in Australia. While the project faced several challenges during its construction (which will be discussed in the failure section), the procurement process itself was a significant success. The procurement team was able to procure highly specialized materials and services from international suppliers to meet the architectural vision of the project.

A key factor in the success of the procurement process was the early involvement of key stakeholders. The design and procurement teams worked collaboratively from the very beginning, ensuring that the required materials were sourced with the highest standards of quality. Despite the project's overall budgetary challenges, the procurement team effectively managed supplier relationships and delivered the high-quality materials and services that contributed to the Opera House's iconic status.

Another important success factor was the flexibility and adaptability shown by the procurement team when faced with unforeseen circumstances. For example, when the original supplier for the concrete was not able to meet specifications, the procurement team quickly identified and qualified an alternative supplier, ensuring minimal delay to the project.

Failure: The Denver International Airport Baggage System

A stark contrast to the Sydney Opera House is the Denver International Airport (DIA) baggage handling system project, which serves as a cautionary tale in procurement. The project, originally envisioned as a state-of-the-art automated baggage system, faced significant procurement-related challenges, leading to delays and cost overruns.

One of the main procurement failures in this case was the lack of proper requirements definition. The baggage system's complexity and the technologies involved were not fully understood by the procurement team, leading to unclear specifications and mismatched expectations between the airport authority and the suppliers. The result was that the suppliers provided technology that did not integrate well with existing infrastructure, causing repeated failures and ultimately a complete redesign of the system.

Furthermore, the procurement team did not fully assess the risks associated with the project. Critical factors such as system testing, coordination between different vendors, and ongoing maintenance were overlooked, and suppliers were not held accountable for these areas, which further exacerbated the issues.

In this case, procurement challenges were compounded by the failure to involve key stakeholders early enough in the procurement process and the lack of a robust contract that addressed the project's complexity.

Analyzing Procurement Challenges in Complex Projects

The Denver International Airport baggage system illustrates how procurement challenges can derail complex projects. When managing complex procurement projects, there are several challenges that professionals must be aware of to avoid costly mistakes.

1. Unclear Requirements and Specifications

One of the most common causes of procurement failure in complex projects is the lack of clear, well-defined requirements. In the case of the DIA baggage system, the project's specifications were not thoroughly thought out, leading to mismatched expectations with suppliers. This resulted in the procurement team sourcing technology that was incompatible with the existing infrastructure.

In complex projects, especially those involving new technologies or untested solutions, it is critical to involve all stakeholders early and define procurement requirements in as much detail as possible. A clear understanding of what is needed, including technical specifications, timelines, and quality standards, is vital to avoid issues during the procurement process.

2. Lack of Supplier Collaboration

Effective collaboration between procurement teams and suppliers is essential for ensuring project success. However, in complex projects, communication breakdowns can occur, leading to misunderstandings and poor execution.

For example, in the case of the DIA baggage system, there was insufficient collaboration between the airport and its suppliers. Suppliers failed to understand the system's complexities, and the lack of continuous communication exacerbated the challenges. This highlights the importance of maintaining ongoing discussions with suppliers throughout the procurement process and ensuring that both parties are aligned on the project's goals and objectives.

3. Risk Management in Procurement

Procurement in complex projects involves significant risks. Identifying and managing these risks upfront is crucial to project success. In the case of the DIA baggage system, a comprehensive risk management strategy would have included assessing the feasibility of the proposed system, identifying potential technological risks, and ensuring that all suppliers had the capacity to meet the project's requirements.

Without a proper risk management plan, procurement professionals can find themselves reacting to problems as they arise, leading to delays and budget overruns. Identifying risks at the outset, establishing mitigation strategies, and ensuring that all stakeholders are prepared for potential challenges will help mitigate risks and prevent them from derailing the project.

Applying Best Practices from Diverse Industries

While procurement challenges may vary depending on the industry, many best practices can be applied across projects to ensure better procurement outcomes. By studying procurement successes and failures in various sectors, procurement professionals can apply the following best practices:

1. Engage Stakeholders Early and Continuously

In the construction of the Sydney Opera House, early and continuous engagement with stakeholders, including suppliers and design teams, ensured that the project's needs were met. This best practice applies across industries. In procurement, involving all relevant stakeholders from the start helps ensure that all requirements are clearly understood and that the right suppliers are selected.

In complex projects, involving technical experts and end-users early in the procurement process helps identify potential issues before they arise. Regular communication ensures that any changes to specifications or requirements are identified and managed effectively.

2. Comprehensive Supplier Evaluation and Prequalification

In successful procurement cases, thorough supplier evaluation is key to ensuring that suppliers can meet project needs. In sectors like construction, IT, and manufacturing, evaluating suppliers based on criteria such as financial stability, technical expertise, past performance, and capacity to meet deadlines is essential.

Prequalification processes help ensure that only suppliers capable of delivering on time and within budget are selected. In industries where innovation and technological advancement are key, it is also important to assess suppliers for their ability to adapt to new trends and deliver innovative solutions.

3. Clear Contracting and Risk Management Strategies

The failure of the DIA baggage system project highlights the importance of clear contracting and risk management strategies. In any procurement, especially in complex projects, procurement teams should develop comprehensive contracts that clearly define expectations, timelines, penalties for non-performance, and risk mitigation measures.

Contracts should outline responsibilities for each party involved in the procurement, and a risk-sharing strategy should be established to ensure that all parties are accountable for delivering their part of the project. This includes ensuring that suppliers are contractually obligated to address risks such as system failures, delays, or quality issues.

4. Leveraging Technology for Procurement Efficiency

As technology advances, procurement professionals must adapt by leveraging software tools to streamline procurement processes. Technologies such as procurement management systems, e-sourcing platforms, and supply chain analytics can enhance transparency, improve supplier selection, and automate routine tasks.

In industries where projects are increasingly complex, technology can also help identify bottlenecks in procurement workflows and provide real-time visibility into supplier performance. By embracing digital transformation, procurement teams can make more informed decisions, reduce procurement cycles, and improve project outcomes.

Real-world procurement case studies offer valuable lessons in both successes and failures. While projects like the Sydney Opera House demonstrate the importance of clear requirements, stakeholder engagement, and supplier collaboration, failures like the Denver International Airport baggage system highlight the risks of unclear specifications, lack of risk management, and poor supplier relationships.

By applying best practices such as early stakeholder engagement, comprehensive supplier evaluation, clear contracting, and leveraging technology, procurement professionals can avoid common pitfalls and ensure the success of complex projects. Procurement teams must constantly adapt and learn from past experiences to optimize procurement processes and deliver projects on time, within budget, and to the highest quality standards.

Section 6: Conclusion and Future Trends

25.The Future of Procurement in Project Management

Procurement, once considered a transactional and administrative function, has evolved into a strategic role within project management. As the global business environment becomes increasingly complex, procurement is playing a critical part in ensuring the success of projects across industries. This chapter explores the emerging trends in procurement, how organizations can prepare for a digital and sustainable future, and the importance of continuous learning and professional development for procurement professionals.

Emerging Trends in Procurement

The procurement landscape is undergoing a rapid transformation driven by technological advancements, changing market dynamics, and shifting expectations from clients and stakeholders. Some of the most significant emerging trends in procurement include:

1. Digitalization and Automation

One of the most profound changes in procurement is the move towards digitalization. The introduction of automation and artificial intelligence (AI) is helping streamline procurement processes, reducing manual workloads and improving accuracy. From automated purchase orders to AI-driven supplier recommendations, digital tools are enabling procurement teams to make faster, data-driven decisions.

Technologies like robotic process automation (RPA) are being employed to handle repetitive tasks such as invoice processing and purchase order tracking, freeing up procurement professionals to focus on more strategic activities like supplier relationship management and contract negotiations. Moreover, procurement software now integrates seamlessly with enterprise resource planning (ERP) systems, providing procurement teams with real-time insights into procurement activities, supplier performance, and inventory management.

2. Artificial Intelligence and Data Analytics

The use of artificial intelligence and data analytics in procurement is another key trend. AI can help procurement teams forecast demand, analyze market trends, and evaluate supplier performance more effectively. Machine learning algorithms can predict price fluctuations, detect fraud, and automate procurement decisions based on historical data, thus minimizing risks and improving cost efficiency.

Advanced data analytics can offer valuable insights into procurement processes, such as identifying inefficiencies in the supply chain, assessing supplier performance, and predicting potential disruptions. By leveraging big data, procurement teams can make informed decisions that optimize the procurement process and align with project goals.

3. Blockchain Technology

Blockchain is beginning to make its way into procurement, offering solutions to some of the longstanding issues in supply chain management, including transparency, traceability, and fraud prevention. Blockchain provides a decentralized and immutable ledger, which means that every transaction can be tracked and verified in real time.

For procurement, this means that organizations can have an accurate and auditable record of every step in the supply chain, from the sourcing of raw materials to the delivery of final products. Blockchain also offers enhanced security, which is especially important for industries dealing with sensitive data or high-value transactions.

4. Sustainability and Green Procurement

Sustainability is becoming a key consideration for procurement professionals, particularly in industries like construction, manufacturing, and retail. The pressure to reduce environmental footprints, minimize waste, and source ethical materials is pushing organizations to adopt greener procurement practices.

Green procurement, also known as sustainable or eco-friendly procurement, focuses on purchasing products and services that have a lower environmental impact over their entire lifecycle. This includes sourcing materials that are recyclable, energy-efficient, and produced with minimal harm to the environment. Additionally, companies are increasingly looking for suppliers who prioritize sustainability in their operations, ensuring that their supply chains are aligned with environmental and social responsibility standards.

5. Supplier Diversity and Inclusion

Another growing trend in procurement is the emphasis on supplier diversity and inclusion. Organizations are increasingly recognizing the value of working with diverse suppliers, including those from minority, women-owned, and small businesses. By fostering supplier diversity, companies not only contribute to social equity but also benefit from a broader range of innovative ideas, competitive pricing, and improved supply chain resilience.

Procurement professionals are now tasked with developing strategies to identify and engage with diverse suppliers, ensuring that procurement processes are inclusive and that all suppliers have an equal opportunity to compete for contracts.

Preparing for a Digital and Sustainable Future

As procurement continues to evolve, organizations must proactively prepare for a future that is both digital and sustainable. The following strategies can help procurement professionals and organizations adapt to these changes:

1. Investing in Technology

One of the most effective ways to prepare for a digital future is by investing in procurement technology. Organizations should look for integrated procurement management systems that leverage automation, data analytics, and artificial intelligence to streamline processes and improve decision-making. Investing in cloud-based platforms can also improve collaboration across departments and ensure that procurement activities are accessible in real time.

Furthermore, adopting digital tools like e-sourcing platforms, supplier relationship management software, and procurement dashboards can enhance efficiency, improve supplier communications, and provide greater visibility into the procurement process.

2. Embracing Sustainability in the Supply Chain

Preparing for a sustainable future requires a shift in procurement strategies. Procurement professionals must consider the long-term environmental and social impacts of their sourcing decisions. To incorporate sustainability, procurement teams can:

> Set clear sustainability goals and integrate them into procurement strategies.

> Evaluate suppliers based on their environmental impact, social responsibility, and ethical practices.

> Encourage innovation by working with suppliers to develop sustainable solutions.

> Consider the total cost of ownership (TCO), which includes the environmental and social costs, in addition to the upfront purchase price.

Sustainable procurement practices not only help mitigate environmental risks but also enhance brand reputation and customer loyalty, which is increasingly important to consumers and investors alike.

3. Adopting Agile Procurement Models

In today's fast-paced business environment, the ability to adapt quickly is essential. Agile procurement models, which focus on flexibility, iterative processes, and continuous feedback, are gaining popularity. These models allow procurement teams to respond more rapidly to changing market conditions, disruptions in supply chains, and evolving project requirements.

By adopting agile methodologies, procurement professionals can better manage uncertainty, reduce costs, and improve collaboration with suppliers. This is particularly valuable in industries where speed and responsiveness are critical, such as in tech, construction, and manufacturing.

Continuous Learning and Professional Development

The procurement profession is evolving rapidly, and procurement professionals must continuously adapt to new technologies, trends, and practices. Ongoing education and professional development are essential for staying ahead of the curve.

1. Professional Certifications and Courses

Procurement professionals can enhance their skills by obtaining certifications from reputable organizations such as the Institute for Supply Management (ISM), the Chartered Institute of Procurement and Supply (CIPS), and the Project Management Institute (PMI). These certifications not only help professionals stay updated with the latest trends but also demonstrate their commitment to excellence in the field.

Additionally, pursuing specialized courses in digital procurement, sustainability, or data analytics can provide procurement teams with the expertise they need to navigate the challenges of a digital and sustainable future.

2. Networking and Knowledge Sharing

Procurement professionals should actively participate in industry forums, conferences, and online communities to stay informed about the latest trends and best practices. Networking with peers, suppliers, and industry experts provides valuable insights and fosters a collaborative environment where procurement challenges can be discussed and solved collectively.

Engaging in knowledge-sharing platforms, webinars, and collaborative groups can also help procurement professionals gain fresh perspectives, share lessons learned, and enhance their problem-solving skills.

3. Leadership and Strategic Thinking

As procurement continues to grow as a strategic function within organizations, procurement professionals must develop strong leadership and strategic thinking skills. This includes the ability to analyze data, manage cross-functional teams, and align procurement strategies with overall business objectives.

By honing their leadership abilities, procurement professionals can play a pivotal role in shaping the future of procurement and influencing organizational success.

The future of procurement in project management is dynamic, driven by technological innovations, sustainability concerns, and a shift toward more strategic practices. As organizations move toward digital transformation, procurement professionals must embrace new technologies like automation, AI, and blockchain to improve efficiency, transparency, and decision-making. Additionally, the growing emphasis on sustainability and supplier diversity presents both challenges and opportunities for procurement teams.

To stay competitive, procurement professionals must continuously update their skills, adopt agile procurement models, and engage in lifelong learning. By preparing for a digital and sustainable future, procurement teams can position themselves as key contributors to the success of projects and organizations in an ever-evolving business landscape.

www.ingramcontent.com/pod-product-compliance
Lightning Source LLC
Chambersburg PA
CBHW071025240526
45469CB00006BD/2087